Exploring Japanese Culture
Not Inscrutable After All

Exploring Japanese Culture

Not Inscrutable After All

Nicos Rossides

Foreword by Jan Gordon

Matador
9 Priory Business Park,
Wistow Road, Kibworth Beauchamp,
Leicestershire, LE8 0RX
Tel: 0116 279 2299
Email: books@troubador.co.uk
Web: www.troubador.co.uk/matador
Twitter: @matadorbooks

ISBN 978 183859 334 6

British Library Cataloguing in Publication Data.
A catalogue record for this book is available from the British Library.

Printed and bound in the UK by TJ International, Padstow, Cornwall
Typeset in 11pt Adobe Garamond Pro by Troubador Publishing Ltd, Leicester, UK

Matador is an imprint of Troubador Publishing Ltd

MIX
Paper from
responsible sources
FSC
www.fsc.org
FSC® C013056

If you bought this book thinking it may be useful as a travel guide, tough luck. It is not for you!

Contents

Acknowledgements   viii
Foreword (Jan Gordon)   ix
Introduction   xvii

Chapter 1   Cross-Cultural Patterns   1
Chapter 2   Aesthetics   13
Chapter 3   A Pathway to Mastery   24
Chapter 4   Cool Japan   34
Chapter 5   The Social Dark Side   53
Chapter 6   Business   70
Chapter 7   Language   89
Chapter 8   Literature   97
Chapter 9   Education   109
Chapter 10   The Legal System   120
Chapter 11   Clouds Over Future Sunrises   129
Chapter 12   Unique or Distinctive?   140

Afterword   153
Bibliography   155
About the Author   159

Acknowledgements

I thank Professor Jan Gordon, a long-time friend, and Japan resident, for writing the Foreword to this book and for acting as a sounding board on the fascinating kaleidoscope that makes up Japan's culture.

I also thank my wife Takako, daughter Nicole and brother Orestis for patiently enduring my on and off attempts at developing the perspectives through which I have viewed Japan's culture and for acting as friendly critics of its contents.

Foreword

同じ釜の飯を食う
("We've been through a lot, together")

The Japanese *aisatsu* (greeting) literally reads "eaten at the same trenches" and is an expression heard when two old Japanese friends, nearing retirement, meet up again after an interval and reminisce. My friendship with Nicos Rossides had its origins in one of the "social spaces" common to Japan in the early 1980's, which included that of the Beat poet, Cid Corman's ("CC's Coffee Shop") in downtown Kyoto and a bit later, a jazz bar in Tokyo owned by Haruki Murakami. We initially met at Honyaradō, on *Imadegawa Dori* in Kyoto. This particular café/club, minimally furnished by long wooden trenchers, served as a venue for *gaijin* visiting academics; research students (of whom Nicos was one); and on occasion, relatively bi-lingual Kyoto Japanese students in search of an extra-mural space to informally practice their English.

The space was neither a designated "pick-up" place nor did it embody the concept of a "third space" (between home and work) which, according to Howard Schultz, its founder, was the early philosophy behind the creation of Starbucks. Vaguely literary ("a book hall") as its name suggests, Honyaradō was an international venue where one could speak what the world (but not necessarily Japan) regards as a *lingua franca*, also on occasion hosting poetry readings in different languages. The zone, years earlier, might have qualified as "counter-culture," but was already slightly *retro* while at the same time pointing *forward* to a more accommodating Japan.

The draw was an inexpensive "morning set": coffee, a novel artisanal stone-ground whole wheat bread, an egg, and a slice of fruit or in winter a whole *mikan* rather than the fish-based miso soup common to traditional Japanese breakfasts. English language newspapers, an endlessly looping Bob Marley tape, a board with notices for those in need of language lessons or offering them completed the rather dark information exchange center. Much as one supposes union "hiring halls" did for earlier immigrants to America in need of extra money and Brasserie Lipp did for the philosophers of the Left Bank in Paris, the premises served a social purpose, not entirely acknowledged by its customers at the time.

A remnant of the "students' movement," which had closed Kyoto's universities for a period, Honyaradō was entirely owned by its staff as an entrepreneurial commune. And, like other left-leaning, utopian experiments of the period, the institution disappeared decades later in a fire of mysterious origin. Little did I know then that I would be writing a metaphoric *hors d'oeuvre* (perhaps better thought of as an *amuse bouche*) of Nicos Rossides' kaleidoscopic reflections on Japanese culture, which must have begun there at breakfast, now nearly four decades ago.

Then a post-graduate student at Kyoto University en route to a doctorate, Nicos was part of a group, which included a Visiting Professor, formerly the Director of the Fulbright Program in South Korea; an Australian graduate student of Japanese linguistics; a "hippy" recipient of a Japanese *Monkasho* scholarship (who seldom attended classes, preferring the environment), and the occasional interloping academics on short-stay visiting appointments as was I at the time. Over breakfast, I was coached by Nicos in reading and writing *kanji* sufficient to be able to read the names on my class rolls. He was already the teacher and still is, even while a continuing student of Japanese culture.

Different cultures deploy different "arenas of contact" between the native population and temporary residents who, unfamiliar with the culture, nonetheless share a commercial, ideological, or cultural interest. One historical example for the colonizing expatriate posted to the Orient was the ubiquitous "hill station," still to be found in so many former colonies of the sub-continent and Southeast Asia. Known under various names—*Darjeeling, Simla, Fraser' Hill* and *Genting Highland* (Malaysia) and *Bogor* in Indonesia—these were glorified spots of rest and recreation in the late nineteenth and early twentieth centuries where colonials could take the "mountain air" in retreat from the threat of imaginary or real tropical maladies and their native carriers. Like the expatriate clubs described in George Orwell's *Burmese Days* or E.M. Forster's *Passage to India* with its incompletely understood gossip, these were social refuges with all the trappings of the *familiar*, including board games and cuisine. But these enclaves, as Thomas Mann well understood, were also, even etymologically, sanitariums of sorts, cleansed of the *local touch*.

Honyaradō's morning patrons were not missionaries, nor occupying American forces (with defined ulterior motives), but academics, would-be academics, and those with some interest in Japan who had been selected and partially or fully funded (by research scholarships, visiting appointments at universities, or grants-in-aid) by the Japanese government during a period of newfound affluence. We presumably came in order to learn or convinced our hosts that we had, rather than being in ideological service. We were, in short, curious about an enduring culture rather than imposing or extracting, two features common to both conventional and neo-colonialism(s): the goal was Heidegger's *mitsein*: "being with."

This book is one product of that informal education. In another sense it represents a reciprocation of the original gift of sponsored acquaintance to a country where gift giving and receiving are part of symbolic exchange known as *giri* (social obligations). Its author's literary ancestors in ancient Greece have recovered only with difficulty from the reputation as suspicious bearers of gifts. But the "lenses" that comprise its chapters are also reflective, allowing the reader to see how its author's life has been *re-interpreted* as he interrogates his relationship to Japan.

We both stayed long enough to free ourselves from our initial sponsors, in Nicos' case, a graduate fellowship to Kyoto University, and in my case, the United States Information Agency who co-sponsored my first trip with a two-week lecture tour on American Post-War fiction. After receiving his doctorate, Nicos became an executive of an international research company and progressed through the ranks to assume leadership positions at firms with a global footprint. Fluent in English, Greek and Japanese, he was a true road warrior, comfortable in different cultural settings. In 1983, when the law was changed, which had previously prohibited the full-time, permanent employment of non-Japanese citizens at Japanese National Universities—private universities always had a cohort of non-Japanese, often missionaries, on their permanent faculties—I was one of the first six nationwide appointments, rather weighted then to specialists in earthquake theory and detection. As the beneficiary thereby of Japanese "affirmative action" initiatives at a particular time, our *debt* to the culture continually maintains a high *interest*, to mix economic metaphors.

There is a similar pattern in our histories. Both of us were supported at crucial stages of the journey and slowly participated in a cultural dialectic. "Managed sovereignty" designed to enable us to "stand on our own feet"; expanded institutional assimilation; followed by marriage, both literal and symbolic, to the culture. This (hopefully) might track the trajectory of other forms of growth available to the intellectually and spiritually curious. Given the *senpai/kōhai* relationships, which define a culture that privileges seniority, the *gaijin* is perhaps a perpetual apprentice—always the student. But if one has opted to be a lifetime student, as Nicos Rossides has, he has good company in Japan where apprenticeship is democratized as a universally shared experience. If one awakens before dawn and journeys to Kyoto's *Ryoanji* (a Zen Temple), he will see ageing novitiates raking the world's most photogenic rock garden into its patterns: aesthetic discipline is a faith.

In an age punctuated by the rich "homeless" with myriad mansions serviced or rented out in their absence on the one hand, and the impoverished "homeless" seeking asylum or participants in economic migration on the other, we students had sufficient means, insatiable curiosity, and a continuing interest in learning for its own sake. In a Japan in which most are hard-working middle-class citizens with their basic needs fulfilled, we had what many Japanese did not: free time to learn and reflect. This book is a cluster of intersecting reflections in a rotating looking glass. In the age of Brexit, proposed walls, and enhanced anti-immigrant sentiment, Nicos' experience foregrounds an alternative exploration of the whole question of sovereignty for wandering academics, spies, diplomats, and international businessmen.

Years ago, in a graduate seminar at my university, I had asked my students to discuss the relationship between narrative, political, and personal sovereignty in Joseph Conrad's *Nostromo*. The author, detached by a pen name, a life spent largely adrift at sea and the use of the spectral "Marlow" as a narrative surrogate was an exemplary exile, or so I thought. Like Nicos Rossides' legendary Greek compatriot, Ulysses, these wanderers become so much a part of all that they meet that there is a persistent danger of losing the self. When I asked one student, to define personal sovereignty for himself, he answered, "my own leased airplane with my logo on its tail assembly." Years later, viewing a future US President disembarking from the same icon, I thought of this as an early "selfie" with all the emptiness of dispossessed modern life. But the Japanese were there first with *karaoke*. Perhaps it has been superseded at the other end of the spectrum by the mobile phone of the stateless refugee with 50 hours of paid-up (empty) time: empty sovereignty.

In his *Being Singular Plural*, the French philosopher, Jean-Luc Nancy, has advanced "touching" as opposed to "knocking" as an intriguing form of social intercourse insofar as it deploys the French self-reflexive in a transitive way: *se toucher toi* is "to touch myself in touching you," but also "to touch you touching myself." The "oneself" is just as indispensable as the "you." Touch exposes insofar as it gives exposition to the one who was not previously seen or heard. The same touch can both awaken and threaten an aspect of the self previously unacknowledged, making us acutely aware of our singularity, but also of another, plural potential. Touch provides a notion of both boundlessness and its limitations of entities related to, yet separate from, each other, as opposed to the loud knock of Commodore Perry's black ships which opened Japan to the west.

For members of "Red Sox Nation," the Neil Diamond composition "Sweet Caroline," sung at the 7th inning stretch at Fenway Park, given familial jinxes and resurrections, may be as relevant as abstract French philosophers. Written for Caroline Kennedy after the death of her father, the refrain, is not such a stretch. As Obama's Ambassador to Japan, she threw out the first pitch on opening day for Japanese baseball: from the "stretch."

How do we stretch to touch alien cultures? A very tentative former student enrolled in a course of mine only after saying *eigo-o furete mitai* ("I want to touch English"). As if the language had a superficial ("squishy") texture in a country that values textures in so many cultural expressions, she wanted to "feel" for its cultural texture as a potentially developing "taste" for further engagement or discovery of the limits thereof. As with *natto* (slimy fermented soybeans), now having a pride of place in the new Museum of Disgusting Foods in Copenhagen, language too may represent a limit that resists being devoured.

My own model, borrowed from parasitology, might be the

blurred relationship between *host, guest* and *customer*, blurred in the Japanese *ongyakusan*. Host and guest are mutually dependent, each needing the other for survival. If we lived only our heritage, we could never really be socially alive because our past could never be *lived* life. To be *lived*, it must be continually re-interpreted when faced with the unfamiliar "guest," an etymological derivative, like "host," of the "ghostly." Host and guest feed off of each other in an arena of mutual *hospitality*—a non-obligatory, non-binding community. That state retains what Jacques Derrida has termed *differénce*: a notion that binds *difference* and the possibility of the *deferred* judgment in the same concept. The late French philosopher's Japanese translator, Takao Tomiyama, uses the Japanese *wakeru*, a "division" that is a form of "sharing." Such a community is gracious, welcoming and resistant to sovereignty in the ways Nicos Rossides has lived and speculatively written about.

What follows is nothing less than a department store of cultural and social practices in the Land of Wa. One walks into many retail emporiums in Japan to be greeted by an extraneous doorman or woman bending at the waist as they say, *irrashaimase* ("come in"). They lean politely forward, a near-bow as an invitation—as in this "Foreword." You may not "get it all down," but it promises an exposure to an exposure.

Jan Gordon
Kyoto, Spring 2019

Jan Gordon is an Emeritus Professor of Anglo-American Studies at Tokyo University of Foreign Studies with advanced degrees from Princeton. He was from 1992 to 2000 a reviewer of books on Japan for *Asahi Shinbun* and was a lecturer for the former United States Information Agency/ Fulbright Program in East and Southeast Asia.

Introduction

I spent seven unforgettable years in Japan in the late 1970s and early '80s at a time when the country began to emerge as a major player on the world stage. Japan was ascendant, having shown remarkable resilience after its defeat in WWII, reaching a level of economic development that became the envy of nations around the world. From a beaten, vanquished nation, Japan metamorphosed into an example to admire and emulate.

In 1977, I was offered a Japanese government scholarship to study urban planning at Kyoto University as a graduate student. I accepted without a second thought. I didn't know much about the country at the time, but what I did read about it, and Eastern philosophies in general, fascinated me. Fortuitously, I had come across Ruth Benedict's *The Chrysanthemum and The Sword* and had eagerly read works on Eastern philosophy such as Herman Hesse's *Siddhartha* and Fritjof Capra's headier *The Tao of Physics*.

Arriving in Japan, fully prepared to absorb and learn, I received intensive Japanese language training at the Osaka University of Foreign Studies (*Osaka Gaidai*) after which I began my studies at Kyoto University's Department of Architecture (in the Engineering Faculty) under the direction of Professor Hiroshi Mimura. The initial graduate research turned into a doctorate program as I immersed myself not just in my chosen academic subject, but in local culture.

During my first week in the country, I recall feeling a sense of awe, combined with an unbounded eagerness to experience and learn from this new culture. My first dinner was with friends at a restaurant close to *Osaka Gaidai* where I was to start intensive language training. It was a cozy place with friendly and courteous staff, serving superb food. Our waitress did an impeccable job. Ah, I thought to myself, she's definitely earned her tip. After paying the bill, I left a generous 2,000 yen on the bill tray. As we left the restaurant, the young woman chased after us to give the money back, thinking I had left it by mistake, returning the money with a deep bow. Even after I insisted, she refused again, saying in broken English that it was her duty to serve us.

As this unfolded, I had a flashback to a *maitre d'* at an exclusive New York restaurant who had rather obsequiously accosted me for leaving "only" a US $250 tip (OK, the bill was quite large as I had taken out more than 10 people). After asking if the food and service had been to my satisfaction, he came straight to the point: What I left as a tip was short of the customary 18%+, suggesting that perhaps I re-write the check.

This first Japanese restaurant experience, and others to come, exemplified firsthand the politeness and sense of duty which characterizes the Japanese. Yet, this is all juxtaposed with what some regard as aloofness toward foreigners (especially those from other Asian countries or Africa), and a sense of exceptionalism masquerading as uniqueness, an attitude that often belies strong nationalism, xenophobia, and a decided lack of inclusiveness. Paradoxical, but rather typical of the many contradictions one feels living there.

Early on in my journey to understand Japanese culture, I realized that the Japanese don't let you *in* easily but friendships, once formed, seem to last. Initially, most Japanese you'll meet may be "friendly" yet are rather aloof, distant and somewhat awkward around foreigners, perhaps a general characteristic of people who tend to be reticent. Intimacy and letting go is hard work for most Japanese, especially in the presence of *gaijin*. Yet, as they become more familiar with you and feel more comfortable, they tend to share more by way of ideas, real feelings and opinions: expressing the *honne* rather than constantly using the protective mechanism of *tatemae* (a distinction I shall later explore in more detail). As this may be said of relationship dynamics across many cultures, I'm not sure if I'm offering any real insight here apart from the observation that the Japanese notion of what is worthwhile in life (*ikigai*) seems to be quite consistent with what Aristotle called *eudemonia* (happiness, well-being), a key plank of which is maintaining meaningful friendships. Relationships form, evolve, and may weaken or dissolve over time but they need commitment (built at least partly on shared interests) to sustain them—both in terms of emotional capital and time—as well as the willingness to make trade-offs with other things of value to us. Whence friendships arise is complex and multifaceted but there has to be an element of discovery or learning from each other in a field (or interest) outside our own; but that may not be all. Whatever it is, though, it may also hinge on our own social comfort zone around people we don't know, something that does not come naturally to most Japanese, amplified by their natural risk aversion. While these factors depend on the individual and cultural context, research by Oxford University professor Robin Dunbar (2010) seems to indicate that there is also a more universal dimension, with roots in human evolutionary development.

In fact, Dunbar's research has posited that 150 (what has become known as "Dunbar's number") is generally the outer cognitive limit of stable social relationships. He conceptualizes relationships as a series of "circles of intimacy" starting with 5 (where the relationship is closest and most intimate) to 15, 50 and then 150 (the normative "outer limit"). The inner two layers of our social world (typically comprising our closest 20 relationships) account for roughly 75% of our social interaction time. The more direct and personal, the stronger the bonds become. Absent "time investment," there tends to be the inevitable decay in the strength and quality of the relationship, so much so that getting into a romantic relationship tends to "cost" us a close friendship (by typically squeezing one relationship out, to accommodate the heavy time investment required). So, in Dunbar's research the amount of time investment is strictly finite, placing real limits on the quality (and number) of our relationships. That aspect of relationship building is indeed universal, although there may be culturally specific factors as to how this plays out in people's lives.

Now turning to my own social relationships in Japan, there was definitely a "decay" of sorts once I left the country and had to limit personal contact to the occasional visit and, prior to Skype, phone calls or letters. Apart from my former colleagues, professors and business associates, many of whom have kept in touch to varying degrees, there was my "*gaijin* circle of friends" (like the author of this book's Foreword) as well as a number of Japanese whose lives became intertwined with mine for several decades. Among those were two families whose lives continue to matter to me (and I presume mine to them) beyond the mere exchange of holiday cards. I got to know both couples (all of them medical doctors) while at university. The relationship(s) with the Isobes (and their two sons) and the Nagaharas (two daughters and a son) had started rather "transactionally." I acted as an English language tutor for the children and provided occasional translation and editing to one of the spouses when she published her medical papers in English language medical journals. But the relationships lasted well beyond their transactional origin. Both families lived in a leafy neighborhood in Sakyo-ku, very close to the university, on a hill-top *cul de sac* accommodating three spacious homes. Both sets of parents had successful careers in medicine. In the Isobe family, the husband was a surgeon, while the wife taught and carried out research at a medical school before setting up her own medical practice. Dr. Nagahara, on the other hand, ran a popular clinic in Kyoto that targeted geriatric patients, while his wife was an ophthalmologist at a local hospital. Both families frequently invited me to their home (they are next door neighbors) and shared many a lovely meal over the years. Even after I left Japan, we stayed in touch (admittedly in fits and starts, with life events such as the birth of a grandchild triggering a "re-ignition" of sorts) and I made a point to visit them whenever possible during my subsequent travels. We recently even connected via Facebook (OK, not with the parents directly but through the kids, who got married off and formed their own families). Over the years, we spent enough time in the company of each other to have shared stories like when I got an acting role as an "extra" in a Japanese film where I played the foreign (Portuguese?) villain whose flirtation with a beautiful Japanese princess drew the ire of a fearsome samurai. Both sets of families went to a half-empty cinema to watch me perform but to my eternal embarrassment my role was confined to a mere 2 minutes! The families had to endure watching a run-of-the-mill *samurai* movie of dubious quality as an obligation to their *gaijin* friend. What is friendship if it is not (at least partly) the cumulation of shared stories and experiences—even embarrassing ones. My foray into the somewhat lucrative world of part-time acting while pursuing my doctorate did not end there. I also got a role as a "bad guy" in a "cowboy" (western) movie, only this time my appearance was literally 10 seconds (enough time to get shot multiple times and to earn a cheque that for most people would have been more than a month's wages). *Gaijin* "extras" (even those with undistinguished looks) were sought after in those days (late 70's), a distant memory given the rising expat population of today's Japanese large cities.

Of course, my goal in writing this book is not to dwell on differences between Japan's culture and that of other countries.

Instead, after gleaning some lessons from Japanese history and examining cross-cultural patterns, I would like to enter some select "windows" or lenses through which modern Japan can be explored and better understood.

For centuries, the Japanese have displayed an exceptional ability to selectively study foreign cultural systems and institutions and adapt them to their own culture. "*Adopt, adapt,* and become *adept*" was a pattern they perfected. The context for this mattered greatly (and still does): A geographically isolated nation, ethnically and linguistically homogeneous, always wary of "the other," but recognizing the need to borrow and adapt so as to grow and prosper.

This began in the early centuries when China provided the cultural inspiration, written language, etiquette, and religion. Hundreds of years later, after a particularly turbulent feudal period (remember the movie *Shōgun?*), the Meiji Restoration arrived, marking a key phase in Japanese history and societal development.

Then came the world war and post-war reconstruction, which marked a huge effort to recover from near-total devastation. All large cities (with the exception of Kyoto), industries, and transportation networks were severely damaged and acute shortages of food were a fact of life for several years. The Allied Powers, under General MacArthur, occupied Japan until April 1952, putting in place a new constitution in 1947. The venerated emperor was stripped of all effective power, although he still acted as a symbol of the state. The new constitution was very much anti-militaristic in spirit— it forbade even the existence of a standing army (though the so-called "self-defense force" provided rudimentary defense, a role it continues to have today). This huge saving was channeled into productive investments as was the case in say post-war Germany but in contrast to modern Greece, which for years spent 5% of its GDP on the military (spending its budget on F16s rather than productive investments).

After the Korean War, Japan began to rebuild its economy, which led to a steady rise in living standards until it faced its first major post-war shock during the 1973 oil crisis. What was a heavily oil-dependent Japanese economy had to veer toward high-tech, creating the foundation for rapid economic growth in the decade that followed.

In the space of 70 remarkable years, Japan moved from a feudal system to a modern industrial economy based on liberal democratic norms. What set the country apart from other historical examples of revolutionary change (such as the French and Russian revolutions) was the fact that there was no drastic change of control between classes accompanied by bloodshed.

The eminent sociologist and Princeton professor Marion Levy (1996), when commenting on Japanese social structures and change, noted that during the country's modernization, the shift of social control was marked by changes in the balance of power between existing social groups—not, as in the West, a shift in control between classes. Significantly, this provided some inherent stability and cohesion, avoiding the chaos of revolutionary social change.

During the 1970s and 1980s, the country had a huge positive trade balance, as a result of a deeply embedded savings ethos. The yen was strong, and Japan was recognized as the world leader in manufacturing and consumer goods. Japan's consensus decision-making system produced efficiency and effectiveness that was essential in the new speed-based economy. As I will argue later, however, Japanese companies continued to operate under this philosophy, at a relative disadvantage, when macroeconomic conditions took a turn for the worse. A slow cumbersome consensus-building system is not ideal when you are experiencing a severe slowdown. When growth slowed, the flaws in the system became starkly evident.

The mid-'70s to mid-'80s marked a period of strong growth, and in some sectors, global economic dominance. Soon after, Japan came to dominate the global electronics industry, manufacturing most of the world's consumer electronics, and introduced new, and in many cases, revolutionary products such as the pocket transistor radio, the VHS recorder, and perhaps the most popular of all, the Sony Walkman. Japanese manufacturers also established a strategic foothold in the growing computer hardware industry, virtually monopolizing the market for semiconductor chips, circuit boards, and other computer components—nearly everything except for CPU chip production, where American companies continued to own the market.

A similar situation unfolded in Japan's automotive industry, which began by offering lower-quality, largely retro-engineered models and then moved to global dominance, in a span of decades, through steady improvements in all aspects of design and production. Focus, consistency, and detail-oriented engineering became synonymous with Japanese car manufacturing, not an easy feat in light of German manufacturing prowess. Further accelerating growth was the rapid increase in domestic demand and the expansion of Japanese car companies into global markets in the 1970s.

External factors and macroeconomic conditions also played an important role. Japan's current status as the world's third largest producer of cars (behind China and the US) can be traced back to World War II. As the country struggled to recover from the effects of the war, its government encouraged smaller vehicles, called *kei-cars*, with limited engine size and dimensions. The resulting vehicles—small and unattractive, but functional in the most basic sense—had to fight to win customers' hearts. But they may have laid the blueprint for how Japan's automotive industry could thrive in the future. Many of these *kei-cars* used technology that had been perfected in the development of small tractors used in small-scale family-owned farms in the period after World War II. Hence, new applications were not entirely separable from the earlier "copycat" versions of American compacts like the ill-fated Chevette.

Michael Cusumano (MIT Sloan Management Review, Fall 1988) carried out extensive research on Japan's automotive industry and described the key stages through which it evolved:

> *Relying on a series of process innovations pioneered at Toyota in response to the small but highly competitive Japanese market, Japanese companies equalled their U.S. and European competitors first in physical productivity. Then they continued improving their manufacturing processes, along with product designs and subcontractor operations. The result was that by 1980, many American and European companies lagged so far behind in productivity and quality that they were no longer competitive. U.S. firms also cut back on design programs that might have led to more popular smaller cars, and procured less costly components, with the result that the variety and overall reliability of U.S. vehicles suffered.*

The blueprint for the success of Japanese firms was to introduce reliable and increasingly stylish products at low prices, beating most US and European manufacturers in the process. Only a few European producers could effectively compete, albeit in fairly narrow market niches.

Indeed, the Japanese did not just copy and adapt. They responded to specific market needs, using techniques first developed in the US in new and innovative ways, creating better overall solutions. In doing so, they set new standards of efficiency and continued to do so, even when the goalposts kept moving toward technologies of the future.

A CNN article (November 1, 2017) about *Why Japan may be the world's next car superpower* argues that the Japanese auto industry is likely to lead the charge globally.

But the allure of novelty shouldn't distract us from a more serious prospect: With automobile design poised to evolve more in the next 20 years than in the previous 50, it is perhaps the Japanese who are best positioned to exploit new demand for connected cars, fuel efficiency and autonomous transport.

Of course, Japan isn't all cool cars and excellent electronics. Its influence went way beyond manufacturing prowess to include areas which fall in the domain of culture. How then can we really view its rise? In my analysis, I choose to view the society through specific lenses (and not the ones you'll see for sale in Tokyo's flashy Akihabara district) that allow us to examine its distinctiveness in more detail and hopefully provide some answers on how it came to punch way above its weight both economically and culturally.

Chapter 1

Cross-Cultural Patterns

As I immersed myself in all things Japanese while taking an intensive Japanese language course, I learned that subtle gestures, facial expressions, and nuanced vocal tones mattered more than what was actually said. But it took a long time before I became passably adept at deciphering intentions, and appropriate ways to respond. What is more, many of the things that one experiences first-hand are only later digested as fitting a kaleidoscope of different nuances and perspectives. To the extent that "seeing" sometimes requires a detachment that comes from looking at something from the outside in, I'm reminded of the Japanese proverb *tōdai moto kurashi*, which literally means "the lighthouse does not shine on its base." It alludes to the difficulty of seeing what is in front of our eyes or put differently, it refers to the ease with which we overlook important things that are right in front of us. So, it is decades after I had actually lived in this lovely yet complex country that I decided to attempt a detached analysis of the different ways we can view Japanese culture.

Edward Hall, an early cross-cultural research scholar and author of several books on culture including *Beyond Culture*, *The Hidden Dimension* and *The Silent Language*, distinguished between high- and low-context cultures. High-context cultures interpret and convert clues and gestures when communicating, with non-verbal signals playing a vital role. In low-context cultures, including most modern Western cultures, non-verbal signs are less relevant, as there is less reliance on nuance and context.

High-context cultures rely on traditions, personal relationships, established hierarchies, and an inherent ability to "read between the lines." Low-context cultures, on the other hand, require more explicit elaboration as they don't have the same depth of tradition, and are perhaps somewhat more prone to shallower, short-term relationships. In high-context cultures, information is either found in the physical context or internalized by the person whereas in low-context communication, most of the information is in the explicit code. High-context cultures require some time to read and re-read (much as do complex, layered literary texts) and these postponements require some patience to accommodate delay. This perhaps partially explains the low levels of violence in Japanese culture. High-context means that there are lots of layered spaces to negotiate before one (often inadvisably) closes the space by some violent act of aggression against the "fly-line" by which all animals are surrounded (see E.T. Hall, *The Silent Language*). This may be a contributor to so-called multi-tasking: one must read an explicit code (common to the allegorical mode with defined symbols of good and evil) and another code ("why is the morning sun in Japan so laden with cultural and legal freight when the sunrise is not radically different from sunrises elsewhere?"). Cultures too have differential "fly-lines" upon which the intrusion of other is read as aggression.

Saying "no" politely is something that the Japanese learn how to do from an early age, creating a space for accommodation and hence the possibility of future deliberation. Ambiguity is welcome and a sign of a person who is accommodating and modest. To the question, "Will you join us for dinner tonight?," they simply reply *Chotto, kyo wa...* Or similarly, *Kyo wa, chotto...*, which loosely translates to "it is a little (difficult)... today," and indicates a simple inability (or unwillingness) to go, with no further need to explain. The word *chotto* can be used when you mean "I would rather not say," as in *sore wa chotto*. Another example of ambiguity is the word *ichiyō* (いちよう)—widely used when we don't want to be direct (denotes "for now" or "at least") and prefer to engage in what I would call constructive ambiguity. "Will you graduate this year?" may be a straightforward question but you could easily get *ichiyō* as a response to avoid communicating certainty (and possibly assertiveness). These plain phrases are usually accompanied by suggestive body language, typical of high-context cultures.

Another widely used cross-cultural framework is the one developed by Geert Hofstede, a Dutch social psychologist. He has become one of the most widely read, albeit rather controversial, authors on intercultural research. Hofstede's *Culture's Consequences* (2001) is one of the most comprehensive analyses of his proposed cultural dimensions. His original bipolar framework to analyze cultures involves four dimensions, adding two more at a later stage. He defines culture as "the collective programming of the mind that distinguishes the members of one group or category of people from others." Hofstede's original study on employee values and perceptions used data collected from IBM's offices in 64 countries. Detailed initial analysis and subsequent surveys on the topic began to show a "global structure" that couldn't be explained merely by the idiosyncrasies of individual countries.

His cultural value dimensions are: power distance, individualism vs. collectivism, masculinity vs. femininity, and uncertainty avoidance. Long-term orientation and indulgence vs. restraint were dimensions that were added later. Applying Hofstede's framework to Japan yields some intriguing insights.

Power Distance
Japan has many characteristics of a hierarchical society. The Japanese are very conscious of status and hierarchical position,

and their language and actions clearly convey the required cues. Position is relational rather than merely self-defining, be it within a corporation or in daily life and is hence part of one's "name." There are "age-appropriate" ranks for various section chiefs (*Kakaricho, Kacho*, etc.), which appear beside the individual name on the *meishi* (name card) so that the two are inseparable even at the first encounter. Each company or even university often has a wearable insignia or distinctive logo, which collectively make up a kind of uniform, much as the shirts worn by IBM staff came to be known as "IBM Blue" in the 1960s. Hence the corporate identity is literally embodied in Japan. Even young women bank clerks and tellers wear identifiable (often designer) uniforms at work. However, we need to take this with a grain of salt, as there are other elements in the mix that make Japan less hierarchical than, say, Korea. In business contexts, decision-making may be painstakingly slow: social accommodation—even if temporary—is valued over a hasty, potentially disruptive response. All the decisions must be confirmed by various hierarchical layers and finally by top management (typically headquartered in Tokyo). But this process (*nemawashi*) may actually point to a measure of egalitarianism and meritocracy, juxtaposed on a strict hierarchy, given multiple informational inputs.

Indeed, there is a strong meritocratic streak in Japanese society that the education system strongly reflects. Everybody can progress if they work hard and do well in school, although, as I'll argue later, there are advantages associated with being raised in a family that can afford expensive private schools and tutors. There is no denying the fact that such investments tend to yield real dividends. Elite universities like Tokyo and Kyoto (Japan's version of Oxford and Cambridge, or "Oxbridge") welcome students from all walks of life, not just the elite, whose advantage tends to be more indirect. When considering applications at public universities, merit (exam scores) is the sole criterion unlike say Harvard or Princeton where "legacy" (having one parent who graduated from there) plays a significant role.

Individualism Versus Collectivism

Japanese society shows many characteristics of a collectivistic society, such as putting group harmony above individual opinion or preference. "The stake that sticks out gets hammered down" (出る釘は打たれる, *deru kugi wa utareru*) is a popular adage that conveys that point most tellingly. What's more, the Japanese have a strong sense of shame ("losing face"). Yet they are not as collectivistic as most of their Asian neighbors. It could be argued that the disarmament following the "end of hostilities" (as the Japanese termed the peace treaty that concluded World War II) had the effect of converting a hierarchical, militaristic, command culture of individual sacrifice directly upon an economic platform of export-oriented industrial imperialism. Yukio Mishima's novels and ritual suicide may suggest a sense of betrayal as a consequence of the imposed conversion from a military to an industrial code: another fear, like that of President Eisenhower of an agglomerative "military-industrial" complex.

Perhaps a manifestation of the collectivist ethic in Japanese culture is the way in which society views glory in failure if it exemplifies adherence to fundamental virtues. Indeed, the co-existence of a focused pursuit of success, with the acceptance of defeat as something noble and heroic, was analyzed by the late British historian Ivan Morris in his classic *The Nobility of Failure*. The heroes Morris talks about refused to make the messy compromises required for success. They failed, but did so in a noble, glorious way (Morris, 1975: xxi):

> *Our red-toothed, red-clawed world, attuned to the struggle for survival and dominance, reveres success, and its typical heroes are men and women whose cause has triumphed. Their victory is never*

without travail, and often its price is the hero's life. Yet, whether he survives to bask in the glory of his achievements [...] or proudly dies [...] the effort and sacrifice will, in the most pragmatic sense, have been worthwhile.

There are distinct facets of this struggle against the odds and heroic failure in Shusaku Endo's novel *Silence* where he tells the story of Catholic missionaries and their converts (*Kakure Kristian*, or "hidden Christians") who suffered brutal repression in 17th-century Japan. Endo himself was a Catholic, a choice dictated by material needs, which created an inevitable personal conflict between his faith and his Japanese heritage (seen by many as necessarily antithetical).

A more recent example of dignity in defeat was the way Japanese players and fans behaved during the 2018 World Cup in Russia. They conceded a goal in the dying seconds of the game against mighty Belgium, yet the traveling fans took time to clear up the stands before leaving—as they had done at each of their four games in Russia. Ditto for the team, who despite their heartbreaking elimination in the most dramatic of exits, cleaned their changing room to perfection. They even left a thank you note in Russian.

If we view this attitude toward defeat from the perspective of culture (the emphasis on conformity, and putting the group above self), it's not hard to see that what appears contradictory isn't so at all. It merely shows how Japanese culture celebrates certain fundamental virtues, among them sacrificing self for the collective, even when the result is catastrophic.

Masculinity Versus Femininity

A high score on this dimension indicates that the society is driven by competition, achievement, and success (typically masculine traits)—a value system that starts in school and continues throughout one's life.

A low score on the dimension, toward the feminine end of the spectrum, indicates that the dominant values in society lean towards caring for others and underscore the primacy of what can be loosely deemed as the quality of life. A "feminine society" is where quality of life is in itself a proxy for fulfillment and success, while dominance and aggression are neither desirable nor admirable.

On this point, Japan emerges as one of the most masculine societies in the world (although together with their mild collectivism, you do not see assertive and competitive individual behavior that's often associated with masculine cultures). Rather, competition tends to be between groups. From the young age of kindergarten, children learn to compete for their group, rather than to prove they are the "alpha male." In athletic contests, like tennis tournaments, there is a standing joke that "everyone gets a prize except the contestant who finishes second from last." As a "loser manqué," he could not even join the group of real losers accorded more than a modicum of respect for their trying!

In corporate Japan, employees are most motivated when they are fighting in a winning team against their competitors. The relentless drive for excellence and perfection exists in all aspects of production and delivery, but mostly in "team" contexts. In fact, so-called "workaholism" can be seen as another expression of masculinity. There is a commonly used term for this, *karōshi*, literally translated as "death by overwork." The rather masculine norm of long, hard working hours is perhaps one of the reasons it is still rare that women, with their central family roles to juggle, climb the corporate ladder to C-suite positions. Yet, I have been told by *sake*-lovers that there is a distinction between styles of the beverage not necessarily corresponding to "dry" and "sweet" wines in the West: a "feminine" *sake* popular in the *Kansai* region with a delicately subtle taste and a more "masculine" *sake* made largely of *yamada hikari* rice produced adjacent to the rugged region fronting the Japan Sea in the northwest. Perhaps this real or imaginary distinction might be more traditional than mere fashion: *Hiragana* (literally "flower writing") was initially a cursive syllabary used exclusively by women, before being fully integrated into the *kanji* of Chinese origin (with uniquely Japanese variations) in modern Japanese.

Uncertainty Avoidance

This dimension deals with a society's tolerance for uncertainty and ambiguity. The extent to which one feels threatened by ambiguous or unpredictable situations leads to the creation of beliefs and institutions that are largely designed to avoid them.

Japanese culture is high on uncertainty avoidance, which to some extent can be attributed to geography, and the frequency of natural disasters like earthquakes, tsunamis, typhoons, and volcanoes, but also to an agricultural basis of value. The seasonal dangers of unanticipated crop or fishery failure had to be partially "hedged," to borrow from economic parlance. The Japanese have had to learn to cope with uncertainty throughout their history. It is therefore not surprising that much thought and effort goes into precautionary measures and contingency plans at both public and private organizations. Monitoring and controlling safety at manufacturing plants or contingency plans for town planning authorities or fire departments are systematic attempts at mitigating disasters. Despite this heightened cultural sensitivity and detailed contingency planning, the Fukushima nuclear reactor crisis in 2011 exposed flaws in Japan's public response, found wanting in many respects. Sometimes sh*t happens or so goes the famous slang expression.

Another manifestation of uncertainty avoidance is the strong preference for ritual in Japanese culture. Ceremonial rituals for "purification" prior to commencing building construction serve to reduce feelings of doubt about what is in store in the future.

This tendency also finds expression in the prevalence of a variety of superstitions in Japanese society. Of course, most societies have superstitions intertwined with a variety of practices and phenomena, but the Japanese have taken these to a different level (as do most Oriental societies).

Many of these beliefs have their basis in the notion that our fate is governed by heavenly constellations. Take *kasō* (house divination) as an example, where the alignment of man-made structures with cosmic forces (for tapping into the cosmic *qi*) is the over-riding rationale, but is intermeshed with the codification of certain common-sense rules around siting and orientation.

Indeed, these practices seem to draw on the ancient Chinese practice of *feng-shui* (commonly translated in English as "geomancy") but with principles that seem to have evolved differently over the centuries. In an article I penned in *Ekistics*, an architecture and town planning journal, in 1982, I used the term "ecomancy" to better reflect the focus on *oikos* (house), but still in keeping with the broad principles of aligning our living space to the forces of the universe while achieving *yin-yang* balance and observing traditional siting and orientation conventions.

I see these traditional practices as perhaps expressive of a Japanese architectural tradition that is quite distinct from the Anglo-American impulse to see homes as a private castle; a refuge from the surrounding environment, rather than a conscious yet primordial attempt to blend and align with it.

Long Versus Short-Term Orientation

This dichotomy deals with how societies try to maintain links with their past while accommodating present and future challenges. Societies tend to deal with this existential tension in contrasting ways. Those which score low on this dichotomy prefer to maintain long-held traditions and norms while viewing change with suspicion. Those societies on the other end of the spectrum go for quick adaptation so as to gain an immediate advantage. The Japanese score high on "long-term orientation," which in the corporate world results in an emphasis on growth and long-term viability, not short-term returns. This orientation often manifests itself in high R&D investment even in economically tough times, prioritizing steady market share growth over quarterly profits. According to Hofstede, Long-term Orientation stands for the fostering of virtues oriented towards future rewards, in particular perseverance and thrift, and an emphasis on status, while its opposite pole, Short-term Orientation, stands for emphasis on quick results, the importance of the present over the future and on protecting "face." One aspect of this privileging of long-term perseverance is the Japanese commercial tendency to sacrifice quarterly profit for expanded market share, often condemned as an unfair trade practice in the West.

Indulgence Versus Restraint

This dimension deals with the extent to which people try to control their desires and impulses, and how they're socialized through their upbringing. It translates to relatively weak control ("indulgence") versus strong discipline ("restraint"), perhaps reflected in Japan's traditionally high household savings rates. The culture tends to be one of restraint in contrast to indulgent societies, which tend to accept instant gratification. Restrained societies don't place much emphasis on leisure time as they suppress desire and gratification in pursuit of success. People with this orientation perceive their actions as governed by social norms, and that indulging themselves is somehow wrong, much akin to the Protestant work ethic in parts of Europe.

In fact, according to academic studies, there is a correlation between deferred gratification in young children and later success in life. According to research at Stanford University by Professor Walter Mischel, the children who are willing to delay gratification (remember the famous marshmallow experiment?) had higher academic test scores, lower levels of substance abuse, better responses to stress, better social skills, and generally higher scores in a range of other life measures.

Beyond Hofstede's work, there are numerous studies that explore differences in human behavior and attitudes in a variety of contexts. These touch upon a wide array of perspectives spanning from political economy, social norms as well as literature and artistic expression. There appear to be clear differences even though there are countervailing "homogenization" forces that may reflect the effects of mass media (especially press and TV) as well as social media, a pervasive influence in an increasingly digital age. These tend to propagate similar notions of what constitutes appropriate behavior in a multitude of areas such as parenting, education, artistic expression and gender relationships. Methodologically ensuring that these pick up cross-cultural (as opposed to intracultural) similarities and differences is not easy. Distinguished anthropologist Ruth Benedict (1934), who saw cultures as integrated wholes wherein the parts coalesce around certain basic values, cautioned that it can be quite misleading if we extract parts from the wholes, compare them (out of context) with parts extracted from other cultures, and then conclude that we have found cross-cultural similarities or differences.

These include specific contexts such as the use of mobile phones and how that varies across cultural contexts. Baron (2010) examined the cross-cultural patterns associated with mobile phone use in Sweden, US, and Japan, noting differences in a group of variables such as: quiet in public space, personal use of public space and tolerance of self-expression. His research touched upon the perceived appropriateness of using mobile phones in various social contexts and explored what respondents liked or disliked about having a mobile phone. The analysis pointed to a number of culturally associated differences, as well as a shared conflicting attitude towards the advantages and disadvantages of reachability by mobile phone. This and similar research probes the question of whether (and to what degree) cultural patterns shape the way people behave in certain contexts.

My exploration of cross-cultural patterns while far from exhaustive provides us an initial, albeit tentative basis, for examining the kaleidoscope that makes up Japanese cultural practices.

We shall now attempt to examine Japanese culture in more detail through a number of specific lenses, starting with Aesthetics.

Chapter 2

Aesthetics

The Japanese aesthetic encompasses a wide array of art forms, extending to architecture, interiors, landscapes, and even the way food is artfully served. Aesthetic principles extend back centuries and draw on a number of traditions and ideals, including those of imperial China, which blended into a characteristically Japanese aesthetic over time. These included the notions of *wabi sabi* (rustic beauty), *mono no aware* (fleeting, ephemeral yet transcendent beauty), and *ma* (empty or formless beauty), and encapsulated a distinct attitude (one could say reverence) toward nature. It informed poetry and calligraphy, the principles around artistic rituals such the tea ceremony and flower arrangement; and extended to interior and exterior living space. It even shaped thinking on art forms such as *bonsai*, tiny trees exquisitely shaped as miniature representations of reality. Then there are the so-called *hanayome shugyō* (loosely translated as "bridal training"), which include: *ikebana* or flower arrangement, the tea ceremony, playing the *koto* (a 16th-century stringed musical instrument). These along with other refined arts have long been considered marks of a dignified upbringing. For young girls, mastering these traditional rituals marks a rite of passage of sorts as a way to prep for marriage, with cooking, flower arrangement, and the tea ceremony being pre-requisites.

My own wife spent years gaining mastery in tea preparation, flower arrangement, and playing the *koto*. By the time she was 20, she was accomplished at all three (reaching the highest level but one for a master), a badge of honor for traditional families in Kyoto, even to this day.

Tea Ceremony

The Japanese tea ceremony, also called "The Way of Tea" involves the ceremonial preparation and presentation of "matcha" or powdered green tea. In *The Book of Tea* (1906), the Japanese art historian Okakura Kakuzō explains the obsessive attention to detail associated with this ritual, beginning with cleanliness:

> *One of the first requisites of a tea-master is the knowledge of how to sweep, clean, and wash, for there is an art in cleaning and dusting. A piece of metal work must not be attacked with the unscrupulous zeal of the Dutch housewife. Dripping water from a flower vase need not be wiped away, for it may be suggestive of dew and coolness.*

The "way of tea" or *chadō* is a spiritual experience, rooted in Zen philosophy. It involves detachment from the world around us, in a quest for harmony and inner peace. Once I visited Uji, Kyoto's tea growing region (to the south of the city), and got a brief history of tea growing. Here is where the sencha tea growing method (steamed during processing, thus preserving its natural enzymes) was perfected and now accounts for nearly 80% of Japan's total production. *Sencha* is a "sun-grown" tea variety (as opposed to "shade grown" teas such as *matcha*) and is plucked 3–4 times a year. There are several quality grades, including some which are handmade artisan teas, made in small batches and costing a fortune.

◇◇◇

Tea ceremony.
(Photo by Kent Wang, Wikimedia Commons – CC BY-SA 2.0)

Flower Arrangement

The *ikebana* (literally "flowers kept alive") tradition dates back to the 7th century when floral offerings were made at altars. Later, they were placed in the *tokonoma* display alcove of a home. It reached its highest level of popularity and refinement in the 16th century under the influence of Buddhist tea-masters and has since grown to a widely practiced discipline, especially among the wealthy. Referred to as *kadō*, the "way of flowers," it implies a journey of continuous learning and an attempt at reaching ultimate mastery and perfection. The arrangements are rich in symbolism and sensitive to the seasons and tend to be varied, unexpected, and always meticulous and precise. Adhering to the core tenets of Zen Buddhism and the *wabi sabi* aesthetic, the resultant creations can be breathtaking. According to one estimate, there are literally thousands of different schools in Japan and abroad. One of the most famous and popular is

◇◇◇

Traditional arrangement of Kinka Ikenobō.
(Photo by Gryffindor, Wikimedia Commons – CC0 1.0)

Ikenobō Senei, with its spiritual home in Kyoto's *Rokkakudo* temple. There is huge variation in the tenets as well as techniques used in the various schools—some extremely stylized and rigid, others much more free-flowing and fluid.

Architecture & Interiors

Aesthetic principles such as those embodied in *ikebana* also find their tangible expression in Japanese architecture, interiors, and indeed, the broader patterns of Japanese living space, including gardens and landscaping. As the delineation between public and private space has always been vague (you rarely find sidewalks in traditional settlements), there was a preference for gated entries as well as walls on the property line. Tiled roofs with broad eaves allowed exterior doors to open for ventilation and to let in maximum sunlight, without letting in rain.

Perhaps a unique peculiarity in Japanese settlements is that while streets have no names, blocks do. Houses within a block are numbered according to when they were built, not necessarily in sequence, which may seem counterintuitive to many. In this sense, Japanese houses are much more akin to the British tradition of literally "endowing" the house with a proper name or foundational moment, which courses through even British literary history: *Mansfield Park, Wuthering Heights, Bleak House, Bladesover House (H.G. Wells), and Howards End (E.M. Forster)*. The estate is a historical repository of familial value, to be passed on as a legacy. It is also the antipode of what occurs in America, where the ambitious or merely restless heroes, like Huckleberry Finn, "light out for the New Territory" on aquatic or paved roads: Route 66; "Tobacco Road"; the traffic accident that forecloses the "American Dream" in The Great Gatsby; John Barth's "The End of the Road," or Selby's "Last Exit to Brooklyn." Japan is not a culture of "movers" and "shakers" nor of the house which bears a proper name, but of selective memorialization within a high-context, unified block, where one may instructively lose his way. The *michi* or "way," combining disciplined adherence to a path and enlightening deviations, is one "way" of understanding the novels of Natsume Soseki whose *Michi Kusa* (*Grass by the Wayside*) might be an illustration of the trope.

Traditional houses often had rice paper screen walls (*shōji*), thin translucent panels that slide open. With several sliding panels on separate tracks, much of the wall could be opened to create a flow for the interior, as well as a "layered effect" for sunlight and shadows. This layering or locked effect (as with roof tiles) emphasizes textured surfaces as opposed to spaces demarcated by lines. Two examples might suffice: 1) the accumulated layers, which comprise lacquerware and the nacreous accumulations of cultured pearls; 2) women's clothing designed by, for example, the couturier, Issey Miyake. *Shōji* panels are even used on exterior walls if the walls open to an interior courtyard or garden, and a projecting eave shields the screens from rain. Because the *shōji* is often painted, one pulls aside a sliding, framed landscape to view the natural one outside.

Sliding panels create flexibility in the house layout. The translucent rice paper allows light to enter interiors. At times, *shōji* panels are replaced with hard panels with a jute coating, still offering flexibility and durability, but lacking the translucent quality. Sliding panels are still common in Japanese houses, at least in one traditional room with *tatami* (woven grass) mats, often with an alcove holding pictures of ancestors. This creates a modular space, often re-constituted seasonally (e.g., *amado* or rain doors placed before the rainy season begins) so that the inhabitant recreates periodically his own space. What would be interior decoration in the West assumes a functionality, not unlike that of certain creatures in nature who rebuild their own houses, seasonally.

House interior.
(Photo by Alfonso Romero, FreeImages.com)

Multi-purpose living spaces abound in Japan, at once providing room for sitting, dining, and sleeping. Traditional bedding, a thin mattress called a *futon*, is typically hung on the balcony to air out in daytime, then folded in the cupboard and effortlessly brought out at bedtime. Wood has forever been the preferred construction material (one reason given is its ability to flex during earthquakes!) and is never painted to show the natural grain. No Japanese house (especially in the frigid north) is complete without the traditional *kotatsu*—a low table with a blanket spread over it, and a concealed heating device inside.

I always recommend that friends preparing to visit Japan for the first time stay at a *minshuku* or *ryokan*, traditional forms of hospitality, which serve as alternatives to hotels and embody traditional living patterns. Your futon mattress is neatly laid out while you're at dinner, pairs of slippers are placed in perfect alignment for your return. And be careful not to wear the bathroom slippers when you return to the sensitive straw mats in the bedroom!

Traditional *ryokan* are also a great way to appreciate *wabisabi*, a unique concept that typifies Japanese history and aesthetics. Its essence is that things are perfect in their imperfection, a rather elusive notion to grasp for many foreigners. One way of thinking about this imperfection is that it is strategic. Asymmetry is a crucial feature of Japanese aesthetics. Unlike Renoir's pictorially balanced feathery flowers in their vases, Japanese *ikebana* is never symmetrical: one must read the spaces between the stalks and flowers as part of the composition. In Renoir, there is also *mono no aware*, a closely related concept: the deep feeling that comes from exploring the beauty and impermanence of the material world. The most commonly used word in Japan is *sumimasen*, literally, "we are not finished yet," used as both an apology and accompanying the handshake after a sports contest. It is done, but we shall continue (which means we are not quite done) and therefore have a continuous, unfinished relationship. The memorialization of the inevitable ending is crucial to appreciation in Japanese aesthetics.

Moreover, when Japan launched its 2020 Olympic campaign, it promised *omotenashi*, the traditional concept of hospitality. One impression that strikes any visitor is how clean everything is, with an army of cleaners for every bullet train, station, and neighborhood. Many are volunteers, encapsulating the sense of *omotenashi* as behind-the-scenes hospitality, without any expectation of praise or reward in return. Not expecting a tip similarly typifies this attitude and is something that tends to astonish many non-Japanese.

Miniaturization

It is tempting to attribute certain cultural tendencies solely to geography. If overdone, this could amount to environmental determinism but I see nothing wrong with postulating that certain cultural preferences and tendencies are due at least partly to geographic constraints. The archipelago's mountainous terrain has resulted in fairly dense settlements and a propensity to structure living arrangements in ways that use space with ingenuity. The preference for multi-use rooms and minimal, yet elegant, furniture arrangements have been perfected over the years. It also affects landscape design, with scaled-down symbolic representations of mountains or islands found in traditional gardens. Then there is the art of *bonsai,* which involves growing mini-trees, a painstakingly detailed yet often exquisite art form.

Since WWII it has also influenced industrial design with compact gadgets a distinct Japanese strength. One of the best-known pioneers of this effort in the consumer electronics space was Sony. The tech electronics giant had a strategy focused on developing and marketing next-generation products, defined as half the price and one-third of the weight and size of existing products. Their product range, which included the Walkman, camcorders, mini-discs and cellular phones came to dominate many segments of the consumer electronics market.

At the U.S. National Arboretum..
(Photo by Sage Ross, Wikimedia Commons – CC BY-SA 3.0)

The Culinary World

A popular embodiment of the Japanese aesthetic, is the fantastic food—delicately shaped, subtly colored, beautifully presented, and, in some cases, ritually consumed. Traditional Japanese cuisine referred to as *washoku* (literally "food of Japan") is typically rice, miso soup and a variety of dishes, mostly based on seasonal ingredients (such as root veggies in winter, pickled veggies in summer, chestnuts in the fall). It is well balanced and always intended to bring out the natural taste—no heavy sauces that act as a sensory over-ride of the main ingredients (be they meat, fish or vegetables). *Osechi ryōri*, which is served to mark the new year, is a special treat. It is not only a culinary feast but extremely pleasant on the eye. The colors and ingredients are both symbolic and beautifully arranged and served in artful lacquerware.

I recall one of the first times I was invited to a Japanese home for dinner by a family of two doctors and their three children. There I sat at dinner with my Japanese hosts, the Nagaharas, a family of two doctors and their three children. As I was having dinner with my hosts, I was trying to be as silent as possible while eating my soup. After an awkward silence, I was asked if

◇◇◇

Japanese breakfast, Tokyo, Japan, June 2012
(Photo by Stephen J. Mason, Wikimedia Commons – CC BY-SA 2.0)

I didn't like the soup when in fact I had truly loved it! I later learned that slurping (rather disgusting according to Western etiquette) is linked with enjoyment and a show of appreciation. By all means, slurp when you're in Japan, although that would be rather awkward at London's exclusive *Nobu!* Unlike Chinese culture where chopsticks are used to gather or even to cut food, the chopstick has a dual function in Japan, operating more like a painter's brush which is used to stir the paint (soy, ginger, wasabi, sea salt) and then dip the morsel of sashimi into the sauce before devouring it. The eater then sees the *moriawase* (as if it were a raw landscape) before rearranging it according to individual choice, careful not to "over-improve" the extremely natural culinary estate that is inherited from a master. One assembles the meal as he or she goes along. A crucial distinction in Japan is that between *ten-in* and *yoshoku*: naturally caught fish versus those cultivated by aquaculture.

How natural? I once was dining with friends at a well-known restaurant in Kyoto specializing in *iwashi* (a local sardine), insofar

22

as nothing else is on the menu. They are served as *sashimi*, as tartare, mixed with onions, charcoal-grilled, in fish balls with soup, "tempuraed" (even the bones) in successive courses. During the first course, the remaining head on a filleted fish severed from the body reflexively seized the tip of my chopstick. Freshness persists beyond death on occasion for the consumer as well, given one or two deaths annually from *fugu*, the Pacific Globefish the remains of whose liver, even in the tiniest quantities, is lethal. Though only quite recently, Japanese aquaculture has developed a *yoshoku* (cultivated) *fugu* hybrid that supposedly eliminates the toxicity at a slight sacrifice in taste.

Chapter 3

A Pathway to Mastery

Mastery of anything in life—art, cooking, or sport—requires painstaking effort and countless hours of practice. No culture has bragging rights in this regard. Mastery, whether largely inherent or cultivated through relentless practice, can be found in all cultures. In Japan, the route to achieving brilliance is typically through a long apprenticeship, where a student learns from a master. There is a prescribed highly ritualized process, based on the philosophy that you first spend a long time observing a master before being allowed to do even the most basic task. Newcomers to Japan are often surprised to hear of the variety of people addressed as *senseis* (in *kanji*, literally "one who sees ahead," a teacher). When at a social event, I once asked what a particular *sensei* taught, to be told that he taught newly hired bus drivers. The apprenticeship lasts two years after the commercial license has been obtained! Much of Japan's informal educational system, in fact, relies upon a *senpai-kōhai* system in which the *kōhai* is a virtual apprentice, learning a skill from a "master" (*senpai*) before going out on his own. There is a long tradition of this in the country even in art or ceramics, occasionally, but not necessarily, disguised as an "adopted" son.

But the *yoshi* (orphan-figure) may, in fact, be a disciple, similarly assuming the name of some master, as did *Toyokuni II* and *III* from *Toyokuni I* (*Kunisada*)—neither stylistically nor biologically related, but, like other offspring, indebted for support and teaching. This system passes on "experientially acquired" skills to those beneath or beyond the formal education system, often the less privileged. Hence from one perspective, the persistence of apprenticeship in Japan can be regarded as socially and economically re-distributive.

I recall a social gathering of some high-society ladies in Cyprus who had been studying *ikebana*. They invited my wife and me, having heard that she was from Japan and had practised flower arrangement for many years at the largest "school" called *Ikenobo*. To my wife's bewilderment (and my bemusement), most of the questions they asked her revolved around the basic principles and philosophy of *ikebana*. That seemed perfectly logical, though at some point I realized the expectation at the table was that learning the principles and the "why" of how things are done in *ikebana* would actually allow them to create a tasteful arrangement or bouquet (like seeking the "secret sauce" that yields sudden mastery in cooking).

But in Japanese thought, observing, followed by painstaking practice (the difficult "doing" part), is what really leads to mastery, and is inculcated in traditional Japanese teaching methods from *kabuki* and *noh* drama to the tea ceremony, pottery, and the "simple" act of cutting *sashimi* and making *sushi*.

In fact, the same group soon asked my wife to "fix" an arrangement one of them had made. Once she had the equipment she needed (floral scissors, knife, tape, and holder), she went to work, cutting a bit here, tucking a branch there. Following the gasps of admiration at the improved creation came the questions stemming from the expectation that if you could only understand the principles ("the secret sauce" behind her changes), you could then make beautiful flower bouquets. But how exactly do you explain beauty?

If you asked Rembrandt to break down the formula behind his creations, no doubt he would find it impossible to articulate it to any meaningful extent. How do you teach the process of creating a masterpiece, other than by watching the master at work? How can you explain the stunning brush strokes of a master painter or calligrapher? While there are universal challenges in gaining proficiency or mastery in any discipline, the Japanese have addressed it in a highly prescribed manner, through the master-student relationship. In fact, it appears not to be too different from the way Michelangelo and Da Vinci led their own teams of apprentices back in 16th-century Renaissance Italy.

Apprenticeship as a system of education and on-the-job training has strong parallels in Renaissance Europe where ateliers or workshops were headed by a famous master artist who educated and mentored a group of student disciples (the boys even tended to lodge in the master's household as well as share meals). There was a progression from "studio boy" (*garzone*), to apprentice, to journeyman and then to master that took many years, each stage associated with definite milestones, similar to the path to mastery in Japanese culture. Like in Japan, authenticity in the modern sense was not an important issue. A master's signature denoted adherence to a certain standard of quality rather than who actually carried out the work itself (which in the case of large paintings was often a group effort).

A case in point is Leonardo Da Vinci. He was educated in the studio of Florentine painter and sculptor Andrea del Verrocchio. He joined Verrocchio's studio at age 14 as a *garzone*, became an apprentice at 17 and finally a master at 20.

Indeed, the dictum "practice makes perfect" isn't unique to Japan, even if the Japanese have refined and prescribed the process to an impressive degree. It is well-documented, for instance, that the Beatles perfected their music in Hamburg, Germany, where they played day and night together (mostly at strip clubs) developing what would become their hugely successful repertoire. By the time they left

Germany for the UK, they'd played over 1,200 times together before hitting the US in 1964 on the road to global stardom. Most bands today don't perform 1,200 times in their entire careers. The Hamburg crucible is what set the Beatles apart (Gladwell, 2008). What the Beatles and other outstanding performers knew, the Japanese have ritualized and truly embedded in the way one goes about achieving mastery. It has been part of the social fabric for centuries as a prescribed pathway to brilliance and achievement.

Becoming A Sushi Master

I could take any example of the ritualized route to mastery and the principles that apply would be the same. Becoming a sushi chef or *itamae* (literally translated as "in front of the board"—the chopping board on which sushi is prepared) requires years of on-the-job training and apprenticeship, typically spanning five years or more. After this long, largely observation centered period, the apprentice is given the first important task related to making sushi: preparation of the rice (*You Me Sushi*, 2015).

"Slicing fish and rolling rice can't be that hard!," you think as you munch on a tasty piece of *sushi* or *sashimi*. If you think the work of an *itamae* is rather simple and formulaic, you'd be surprised by what is really involved once you observe the process up close. In fact, becoming a respected *itamae* takes precision, commitment, and, most importantly, immersion. So much for just slicing up some salmon! When I once asked why there were no female *itamae* to a woman colleague, she replied that because women's body temperature fluctuates during the monthly cycle, the shaped rice upon which sushi is placed would unpredictably vary in cohesion. This may be folklore, but even Japanese folklore contributes to quality-control, "just in time" delivery, and perhaps, but only perhaps, a residue of misogyny that foreigners observe in some Japanese conventions.

An *itamae* is both an artist and a craftsman. Typically, he or she starts in a *sushi* kitchen largely confined to cleaning and other

◇◇◇

Sushi being prepared, Tottori, Japan.
(Photo by David Monniaux / Mai-Linh Doan – Retrieved from Wikimedia
Commons – CC BY-SA 3.0)

menial tasks: washing, scrubbing, but no involvement in the actual preparation. That comes in time, when you are allowed to help prepare the rice used to make *sushi*. This critical ingredient must be perfect—in consistency, flavor, and color—and is prepared every day with vinegar and salt. You make it under the scrutiny of your *itamae* until he or she is satisfied that your work meets the highest standard. Keep producing flawless rice day after day, while performing menial duties diligently, and you may progress to the rank of *wakiita*.

Wakiita literally means "near the cutting board" in Japanese— one step closer to becoming an *itamae*. At the *wakiita* stage, you're finally allowed to use your own cutting knife or *hocho*. These come in a variety of shapes and sizes and are designed to slice *sushi* ingredients with precision. Extremely sharp and traditionally made from high-quality carbon steel (the same material used to craft a samurai's *katana*), *hocho* are a critical part of a sushi maker's toolkit.

After years of apprenticeship, followed by years as a *wakiita*, you may finally become an *itamae*. Most will have spent between five and ten years of immersion to achieve the required level of mastery for that distinction. Again, there is no way to shortcut the process.

Of course, with the inexorable progress in artificial intelligence, culinary and other artisan crafts are giving way (for now, rather slowly) to industrial forms of production. Kawasaki (of motorcycle fame) has a robotics division that is manned by sushi-making robots. They can assemble thousands of *nigiri* per hour, way faster than the artisan way of doing it. The robot uses one hand to place the *wasabi* on a thin bed of rice held by the second hand and then adds the tuna or shrimp. Voilà, your delicious sushi is ready to eat!

Reaching Mastery in Sumo

The Japanese approach to mastery naturally extends to the world of sport. The same ritualized process and basic principles apply. The master-apprentice relationship (or its variant *senpai-kōhai* or senior/junior ranking) again is key. Observe first, only then do. And in the case of *sumo*, this follows a predictably prescribed path.

Sumo offers centuries of tradition interlaced with the *Shinto* religion. Highly ritualized, *sumobeya* or "stables" is where the wrestlers live, eat, train, and sleep during their careers—unless they marry, in which case they're allowed to live in separate quarters. A typical stable consists of 15 wrestlers and is hierarchical, always adhering to a detailed and strict code of conduct.

The wrestlers in a given stable are ranked in a pyramid-shaped hierarchy. A winning record moves you up in rank, while losing moves you down. Lifestyle and social protocol inside and outside of the *heya* is based on your rank. The top five spots are collectively referred to

◇◇◇

Sumo fight in the Kokugikan in Tokyo, Japan.
(ElHeineken, Wikimedia Commons – CC BY-SA 4.0)

as the *makuuchi* division. The highest rank is that of *yokozuna*, or *sumo's* Grand Champion. Only a few wrestlers reach the pinnacle. Right below the *makuuchi* division is *juryo* (where you are effectively a salaried professional), a status only one in ten wrestlers get to. All other ranks below *juryo* are still apprentices. Apart from their monthly salary, *juryo* also enjoy bonuses and perks, such as being allowed to marry, have assistants, and wear a *kimono* and *mawashi* (a special belt).

There are two paramount factors in sumo: your performance in the ring and how you behave, in both victory and defeat. Demeanour matters greatly as conveyed by the term *hinkaku* (the embodiment of grace, dignity, and quality of character). This is an indispensable virtue among sumo wrestlers, an absolute must before a wrestler can make any progress. The highest rank of *yokozuna* is awarded on the basis of how much power and *hinkaku* a particular wrestler is judged to have.

At any moment, there can be several *yokozuna*, or none. It's a title that can't be lost, as holders are expected to retire from competition when they no longer perform at the highest level. The Japan Sumo Association (JSA) recognizes 72 *yokozuna*, dating back to the 16th century. All were Japanese nationals until 1993 when Chadwick Haheo Rowan, a wrestler from Hawaii (who assumed the ceremonial name *Akebono Taro*), became the 64th *yokozuna*. A few years later, another Hawaiian (*Musashimaru Koyo*, born Fiamalu Penitani) became the 67th. What was previously unthinkable became grudgingly accepted by most Japanese, to the chagrin of some on the far right.

Indeed, the rise of these *gaijin* (literally "outsiders" or foreigners) was not embraced by all in the *sumo* world. To the die-hard traditionalists, the very idea of a foreign *yokozuna* was seen as sacrilege: "They simply cannot embody the *hinkaku* ideal" went the argument, but it was a losing one, as a rising number of foreigners made the coveted grade. Indeed, in the past couple of decades, the success of Mongolian wrestlers fueled an identity crisis for Japan's traditional national sport.

A case in point is that of Mongolian wrestler *Asashōryū* who became one of the greatest *yokozuna* of all time. At the peak of his career, he trounced his opponents, not just defeated them. He was the only wrestler to win all six of Japan's biggest tournaments in one year! Despite his unrivalled success, *Asashōryū* was a constant source of friction and controversy in the *sumo* world, his behavior not deemed sufficiently humble and gracious. The contradiction between his undeniable ability in the *Dohyō*, and his controversial behavior outside it, ultimately led to his downfall. In Japanese sports, there is no clear line demarcating skill, attitude, and public behavior. Taste and conduct are inseparable from mastery: a practice embodied in the history of the tea ceremony, which began, not unexpectedly, among a samurai class, which displayed their weapons, utensils, and ceramics only to those closest to them, and hence entrusted.

Whether you ever come to grips with the nuance of *hinkaku*, attending a *sumo* tournament is a memorable experience. Watching the wrestlers hurl salt skyward to purify the clay ring before fighting, the nimbleness they show despite their huge frame, as well as the way the audience reacts when a grand champion is beaten by an underdog, is a truly memorable experience. But most importantly, it illustrates the inherent dignity associated with winning or losing, rarely seen in sports today. I have never heard of a brawl (or even a disagreement) during a sumo match. The result is accepted without argument whatever the decision.

I chose sumo as an example of how the principles of achieving mastery are applied but the same practices pervade all sports, from baseball through to football (soccer) or tennis. The pecking order followed in *senpai-kōhai* relationships is a fact of everyday life for the vast majority of Japanese athletes, even in sports which gained more recent popularity such as football (soccer). The J. League and Japan's national team (the Blue Samurai) became increasingly popular in the last two decades, attracting a passionate following among the young. In my first year at Kyoto University (way before soccer's popularity took off), I joined a football (soccer) team where due to my longer experience than most players I was seen as a *senpai*—one from whom the younger and less experienced team members could learn. Sadly, in my first game, I suffered ligament damage that ended my short-lived foray into Japan's nascent football world. Nonetheless, the exposure to dressing room and on-the-field etiquette was quite fascinating, bordering on the inexplicable (as when "seniors" treated juniors in ways that I would regard as downright abusive).

It is hard for many Westerners to accept deference to someone merely on account of their seniority, something that comes naturally to Japanese. To us, respect and authority don't come automatically, they are earned, so we may find it difficult to accept the degree of deference they require. In fact, there is a commonly used expression to describe this social hierarchy as it applies to senior high schoolers: "A god in the fourth year, a nobleman in the third, a commoner in the second, and a slave in the first."

To the Japanese, going through a stage that is likened to slavery is viewed as a "rite of passage" of sorts, a necessary stepping-stone on the journey to accomplishment and success.

Chapter 4

Cool Japan

For many years after Japan's defeat in WWII, its image was one of a country populated by hard-working, well-educated, and committed people, willing to make countless sacrifices to catch up with the West. By the mid to late 1960s, the largely impoverished "striver" image morphed into that of an economic powerhouse, which managed to not only catch up but to outcompete the rest of the world. This particular image may contrast with the creativity and "cool" that has come to be associated with some facets of modern Japan. Yet, as with many seeming contradictions I pointed to earlier, it makes intuitive sense to those who've lived there.

Joseph Nye, a Harvard University foreign policy expert, speaks of the importance of soft power in international affairs. He sees soft power as the means to success in world politics, underpinned by the ability to attract and persuade rather than force. He contrasts this to hard power, which is based on coercion and grows out of military and economic might (Nye, 2005).

Similarly, Andrew Rose (2015), in his article *Like Me, Buy Me: The Effect of Soft Power on Exports,* sees soft power in terms of "cultural assets." He cites the example of pop star Taylor Swift and Hollywood blockbusters like *Star Wars* as ways of boosting positive perceptions of America globally, while at the same time increasing demand for related American goods. "Countries are always concerned about their image, but the soft power effect has a very tangible commercial pay-off." The Japanese understood this all too well and went about achieving soft power in a way that was methodical and systematic, driven largely from the top (government).

The rise of Japan as a global cultural force, wielding soft power first in Asia and later across the world, happened to coincide with the so-called "lost decade" of the '90s. It was partly spontaneous but largely planned—the result, at least in part, of a conscious "national branding" effort undertaken by the Japanese government. The clear objective was the increase of influence first in Asia, and then globally. This also involved the erasure or repression of considerable "hard power" exerted by Japan before and during World War II, which had left painful memories in parts of Southeast Asia. The main commercial goals of national branding efforts are typically related to export promotion, inward investment, and tourism. Japan's strategy was no different and one could say more purposeful and systematic than most.

In a *Foreign Affairs* journal article, Peter van Ham (September/October, 2001) discusses the phenomenon of national branding, and makes the point that "Smart states are building their brands around reputations and attitudes in the same way smart companies do." In fact, such national branding efforts, and clever positioning, were largely evident in Japan's successful bid for the 2020 Olympics (Yano, 2009). They fended off challenges by Madrid and Istanbul by not leaving anything to chance and projecting a strong cultural brand. They even got Prime Minister Shinzo Abe to fly in and, while reinforcing Tokyo's strong points, to personally reassure doubters over any health risks from radioactive leaks at the Fukushima power plant. In the final vote against Istanbul, the Japanese won by a wide margin, 60-36.

More recently, the phenomenal success of Marie Kondo's book (2014) *The Life-Changing Magic of Tidying* (which is now a popular Netflix series) was seen by Christopher Harding writing in the *New York Times* (January 18, 2019) as heir to a long tradition whereby "Japan is marketing itself as a spiritual foil to a soulless West." In fact, the title of the opinion piece, *Marie Kondo and the Life-Changing Magic of Japanese Soft Power,* frames Kondo's success as an example of the nation's soft power on the global stage:

> *Japan's mission in the world...should be to succeed where the West had evidently failed: creating a form of modern life that integrates technological with spiritual progress, rationality with intuition and emotion, individualism with a deep feeling for community. As exports went, it beat geisha dolls and paper umbrellas.*

In fact, the notion of *Ikigai* (a word that combines the ideograms for "life" and "worth" or "value") can also throw some light on this philosophical perspective. Loosely translated as "reason for being"

◇◇◇

Marie Kondo speaking at the 2016 RISE conference in Hong Kong.
(Photo by RISE, Wikimedia Commons – CC BY 2.0)

it resonates with those of us who seek more spirituality in an existence that unfolds at a frantic pace and has allowed technology and material wants to overshadow the need for fulfillment, balance and spirituality.

Japanese Food

I've already talked about Japanese food in the context of my broad discussion on Japanese aesthetics. In this lens, as it pertains to Japan's cultural clout across the world, it is one of the most potent symbols of Japanese cultural influence, especially *sushi*. Of course, Japanese food isn't only *sushi*. Many (but certainly not most) Japanese restaurants have become successful despite not emphasizing *sushi* or *sashimi* on their menus. Wagamama, for instance, became immensely popular by specializing in a range of wholesome and simple dishes, including noodles and curries in restaurant formats that are based on the concept of "casual dining" especially appealing to the young and health-conscious. Having said that, some Wagamama franchises across the world could not resist the pressure of including some *sushi* dishes in their menu.

Despite the success of non-*sushi* based menus such as Wagamama's, the fact is that *sushi* has caught on the world over. Indeed, it coincided and therefore managed to leverage the healthy food trend in the West, and became popular with both young and old. *Sushi's* origins can be traced to 3rd century A.D. Chinese writing, which detailed the use of fermented rice as a practical way to preserve fish. The dietary limits of Buddhism helped *sushi* spread to Japan, as people chose fish instead of meat.

Sushi preparation changed drastically over the centuries, with the pickling levels decreasing before ending altogether and swapped for fresh, raw fish. By the 1920s, *nigiri sushi* was served all over *Edo* (modern-day Tokyo). Refrigeration allowed it to spread around Japan by the '70s, while it began to make inroads across the Pacific.

An article in *The Guardian*, *How Sushi Ate the World*, explains how the love for *sushi* spread. It argues that the tasty treat's globalization started in large expatriate Japanese communities all along the Pacific Rim—in the western and southern parts of the US, Australia, and Brazil. After going through their long apprenticeships in Japan, it became a rite of passage for Japanese chefs to go to these outposts and prove themselves in a "less rigorously traditional" context. Nobuyuki Matsuhisa of *Nobu* fame made *sushi* in Lima, Buenos Aires, and Anchorage before he settled in Los Angeles in 1978.

But it was the invention of the California roll that marked sushi's crossover from native cuisine to global delicacy. It's the most typical element of a sushi assortment—a mixture of cooked crab, avocado, and mayonnaise inside a roll of sushi rice, bound with a strip of nori seaweed. (Renton, 2006)

I remember as a young man visiting Tokyo's *Tsukiji*, the world's largest fish market, that was a vibrant part of Tokyo's culinary scene until it was closed for tourists in 2017 to be relocated to Toyosu in October 2018.

Visiting the market was a truly memorable experience for me, the kind that engages all senses: sight, smell, and sound. Hovering above, you could see forklifts loaded with huge tuna that was typically auctioned before sunrise every morning. Due to huge demand, only 120 visitors were allowed to witness this, on a first-come-first-serve basis. I didn't get up early enough to get in, but I did enjoy some extremely fresh *sushi* at the Tsukiji Sushi Restaurant.

Retailing Concepts

Japanese retailers merely copied Western concepts and formats for years. In the mid-1990s, my wife and I met a couple in London who explained that the husband's job was to gather intelligence on retailing best practice and send it back to his head office in Tokyo (he worked for one of the big Japanese retail chains). These reports covered activities at Harrods, Harvey Nichols, and Selfridges, among others, and covered retail trends, formats, pricing and the like.

No doubt intelligence gathering continues to this day but Japanese retailers increasingly display a streak of newfound creativity and innovation in carefully targeted retail niches. Cases in point are *Uniqlo* and *Muji*, both growing internationally while many Western chains struggle to survive.

Uniqlo follows a philosophy of what they call "LifeWear." Their corporate mission is to "create clothes that make life better." To this aim, they continually research the latest fashions and lifestyles from around the world, looking for new materials that appeal to its young, trendy customers. In a marked departure from American and British apparel retailers who often outsource the production of clothing to second- and third-party contractors in low-wage countries like Bangladesh, Uniqlo operates its own manufacturing facilities in these countries under its own trained supervisors and operators. One result is enhanced quality control and the ability to respond more quickly to fickle changes in fashion (and season) among its youthful customer base. Production would not be different from inventory control insofar as both demand "just-in-time" delivery.

Muji based its success on a no-brand philosophy, which focuses on well-designed, practical houseware, apparel, stationery, and a wide

◇◇◇

Uniqlo.
(Photo by David Pursehouse, Wikimedia Commons – CC BY 2.0)

array of other no-frills products. The brand name literally means "no brand" and was built on the following key principles (apart from its no-logo, no-brand credo): design minimalism, emphasis on recycling, and avoidance of waste in production and packaging. Its marketing mastery seems commercially derivative of one of the tenets of Zen according to the old American quip uttered by a visiting foreign novitiate to his companion during a meditation: "Are you not seeing what I'm not seeing?" Muji's mastery is leaving nothing outside itself, even in its almost invisible wrappers in a country which often overwraps its products for sale. The innovative company is a kind of "Un-cola."

The Fashion Industry
Several Japanese designers have made their mark in the extremely competitive global fashion industry, breaking the perennial

◇◇◇

Muji Store at the Tokyo Midtown Project.
(Photo by Kim Ahlström, Wikimedia Commons – CC BY 2.0)

dominance of French and Italian designers. Each of them has a devout following and have typically graduated from the prestigious Bunka Fashion College, situated among the skyscrapers of Shinjuku business district in Tokyo. It is in this famous design school that aspiring designers first learn about the human body before they immerse themselves into the rest of the curriculum. Dedication to taste and perfection is an absolute must, but as with everything in Japan, one has to take the painstaking steps to achieve mastery. No shortcuts here either.

Several of the alumni who went on to leave their imprint on Japanese design, characterized by avant-garde shapes, high-tech fabrics and a preference for black colors, now have followers across the globe. Some of the best known include *Kenzo Takada* (founder of the Kenzo line of clothing, perfumes, and skin care); *Issey Miyake*

41

◇◇◇

Collage Kenzo
(Photo by NicolleS, Wikimedia Commons – CC BY-SA 4.0)

(famous for futuristic, tech-inspired designs, and his most well-known product, L'eau d'Issey); *Rei Kawakubo* (founder of the Comme des Garçons fashion house) and *Yoji Yamamoto* (known as a "master tailor" whose avant-garde designs incorporated traditional Japanese aesthetics).

On a more general note, Japanese consumers are well known for their passion for luxury brands. According to one estimate, Japanese consumers buy more than $20 billion worth of luxury goods every year and account for half of the total global consumption for luxury brands. In fact, during the 1994–2001 recession, demand in Japan for Louis Vuitton products went up substantially! Even today what have been referred to as "super-rich" are avid consumers of all kinds of luxury goods but they still prefer to do it in a way that is not regarded as ostentatious. In fact, you may live next door to someone very wealthy but their house may not differ much from yours!

By official accounts, a person is defined as wealthy if his or her annual income is over ¥30 million, in addition to having assets of at least ¥100 million. According to this definition, 1% of the population (roughly 1.3 million) falls in this category—quite a substantial number.

TV Series and Pop Music

The penetration (or "export") of Japanese TV programs started in the 1970s, and grew rapidly in the '80s, first in Asia and then globally. In fact, Japan's soft power was beginning to be felt especially in Korea and China, as their youth began to adopt Japanese fashion. The Chinese term "*harizu*" was coined to signify young Chinese who acted as a "Japanophile tribe" by mimicking Japanese fashion and enthusiastically following *anime* and *dorama* (JETRO, 2005). That success was emulated by the Koreans who adopted key concepts from Japan's playbook, giving rise to the immensely successful K-pop. The popularity of Psy's single "Gangnam Style" (billions of

◇◇◇

Members of Momoiro Clover Z, Japanese pop idol group in Japan Expo 2012 in Paris.
(Photo by Dj ph, Wikimedia Commons – CC BY-SA 2.0)

YouTube hits and counting) outdid even the most successful US or Japanese singles. In fact, it was the most watched YouTube video in the world for several years until it was surpassed by Luis Fonsi's "Despacito" which managed to lead the rankings for even longer on the back of a Latin music global popularity wave.

Japanese pop music (known as *J-pop*) had its roots in traditional Japanese music but drew inspiration from pop and rock music in the UK and US. The popularity of female and male so-called "idol" singers and their groups was first felt in Japan itself, but soon some became household names across Asia.

Female singers/songwriters such as Yui and Aiko (reflecting a trend for single name "catchy" branding) have been extremely popular, both domestically and internationally. Namie Amuro, the "Queen of Japanese Pop," also called the Asian equivalent of Madonna (and now retired from the pop world), is said to have broken the stereotype of the youthful idol as she experimented with different music styles and visual imagery, delivered with her soulful voice. Then comes Funky Monkey Babys, an extremely successful trio formed in 2004, characterized by their largely hip-hop sound and high-energy live performances. Widely known as *Fan-mon*, they were also known for having celebrities star in their music videos and jacket covers. Others later followed such as the female idol group Momoiro Clover Z. Formed in 2008, the group was made up of selected members of Stardust Promotion Agency and became very popular with a distinctive style incorporating gymnastic, ballet and action movie elements.

Manufacturing "Idols"

Japan's entertainment industry is a huge business and its appeal extends way beyond its shores. A central aspect to the industry's success is its ability to "manufacture" idols, worshipped by millions of fans. One would think that once "discovered" and established in the entertainment world, that these entertainers would have the upper hand. Often this is not the case, as the real commercial levers belong to the companies to which they are under contract. Yes, the "idol" may amass riches and fame but the commercial reward and power tend to be asymmetric. Indeed, Japan's entertainment industry has a dark underbelly, perhaps to a degree that may surprise even those who are familiar with the unseemly aspects of Hollywood or Bollywood.

A look at this industry shows how the powerful can act as if they are beyond the law. It is reported that they treat their "products" (idols) as disposal commodities, which can be discarded when their "sell by" date expires. Companies and agents tend to act with near impunity because they can ruin people's lives if they don't conform. This leads to a kind of self-censorship or silence typical of the Mafia's *omerta*, but perhaps comparable to the recent claims by American actresses of sexual harassment at the hands of directors, producers, and agents. Celebrities know that in return for fame and money, they are essentially the property of agencies, with no real power or control over their careers. Simply voicing an opinion or resisting an advance can be problematic at best, career-ending at worst. How to retain personal or corporate sovereignty in a world of "agency" is, of course, a problem not confined to Japan, though perhaps accentuated in a hierarchical culture.

Hernon (2016) quotes a popular actor:

> If you say something too controversial, you might get your manager in trouble, so that's something to avoid. It's hard. There are lots of issues I'd like to write about for my blog, but I know there's a limit to what I can say. I've spoken to actors in America who have the freedom to criticize, protest, and speak about elections. We're not able to do that.

So, while the production of idols may be a manifestation of "Cool Japan" in that its international success is undoubted, it does exemplify some rather unseemly aspects of Japan's entertainment business.

The Karaoke Craze

A blend of two words—*kara* (empty) and *oke* (orchestra)— is Japan's unique invention of a sing-along format whereby amateur (and some bad-sounding) singers take the stage to the accompaniment of a jukebox machine that provides the background sound and often the lyrics. It offers a convenient escapist illusion that you have a good voice, while the audience has to endure the cacophony that ensues. The fact that you often make a fool of yourself can be excused on the basis that you were drunk while doing it. The venue of shared suffering is perhaps an apt representation of the spirit of *ganbatte*. On the other hand, just below the surface lurks the perfect device, which allows otherwise reticent individuals to suddenly be stars, at least

◇◇◇

Karaoke in the Irish Pub "The Old Dubliner" in Hamburg, Germany.
(Photo by Hinnerk Rümenapf, Wikimedia Commons – CC BY-SA 3.0)

for one song. *Karaoke* houses are equipped with props, top hats, and fancy clothes to change into—ideal for getting closer to colleagues and customers after hours.

In fact, the karaoke craze began in the early "70s, quickly spread to other parts of Japan and now it would be hard to imagine a place in Asia (or indeed the world) without a karaoke bar. The machine was conceived by a native of Osaka, Daisuke Inoue, who was an avid musician (drummer) in his youth. He did not go through the laborious (not to say expensive) process of patenting the concept, even though he did copyright the name (in the US) in 2009.

Once the original entrepreneurial challenge wore off, and having seen his invention become a global phenomenon, he had a bout with depression, crediting his dog for helping him get through it. In 2004, he received Harvard's *Ig Nobel Prize*, an award that is presented for inventions that "make people laugh—and then make them think." This satiric prize is awarded annually since 1991 to celebrate unusual achievements in scientific research and in this case, it was for "providing an entirely new way for people to learn to tolerate each other."

After accepting the award at Harvard University's Sanders Theatre, Inoue apparently received the biggest standing ovation in the history of the awards. A year later, in 2005, Inoue's feat was the subject of a fictionalized biographical film, predictably called *Karaoke*.

In case you wondered what other unusual inventions have been awarded the *Ig Nobel Prize*, here is a random sample:

- using a simple animal-training technique (called "clicker training") to train surgeons to perform orthopedic surgery
- measuring the degree to which human saliva is a good cleaning agent for dirty surfaces

- demonstrating that wine experts can reliably identify, by smell, the presence of a single fly in a glass of wine
- documenting that most people who use complicated products do not read the instruction manual
- investigating whether it is effective for employees to use Voodoo dolls to retaliate against abusive bosses.

Gaming: PlayStations and Pokémon

Young people the world over become immersed in Japanese youth culture in various ways. The popularity of gaming, especially video games such as Pokémon, has strong Japanese origins. A quote from Talbot (2012):

If you're the parent of an American child, then you may well have noticed how Japanese culture has influenced our kid culture. No set of images has dominated childish desires quite so handily over the last five years or so as the amalgams of cuteness and power in the Japanese-made cartoons (and their many product spinoffs): Pokémon, Digimon, Dragon Ball Z, Sailor Moon, Hamtaro, Hello Kitty, and most recently, Yu-Gi-Oh. It's enough to make Disney envious.

Besides the fact that *Pokémon Go* captured the imagination of kids and adults in every corner of the world, what's truly astounding is the amount of money Japanese gamers spend per download (three times that of their US counterparts). This has made the gaming giants, such Nintendo and The Pokémon Company, commercially very successful. If you add Sony and its immensely popular PlayStation to the mix, these companies have helped establish

◇◇◇

Pokémon Center Singapore at Jewel Changi Airport.
(Photo by Hinnerk Rümenapf, Wikimedia Commons – CC BY-SA 3.0)
INSET. *Costume of Pokémon character, Pikachu.*
(Photo by Tony Hisgett, Wikimedia Commons – CC BY 2.0)

"Cool Japan" and its soft power on the world stage, especially among the youth segment.

Anime and Manga

Anime (from the English animation) and its comic book counterpart, *manga*, have become a multi-billion dollar industry worldwide, no doubt propelled by the explosive expansion of the internet as well as online streaming services such as Netflix and Amazon.

Viewed from a broad communications perspective, they are both effective graphic and visual art mediums for story-telling albeit with important differences. *Anime* (such as *Pokémon* or *Hello Kitty*) is what we refer to as cartoons (TV shows or movies), while

◇◇◇

Anime Expo 2013, Culture Japan.
(Photo by Michael Ocampo, Wikimedia Commons – CC BY 2.0)

manga is a comic book or graphic novel. In fact, *anime* tends to refer to the breadth of Japanese animation, having its origins in the start of the 20th century and is often inspired by popular *manga,* producing animated versions of *manga* storylines.

Manga can be traced back to the Tokugawa period (1600-1868) when illustrated books and woodblock prints attracted intense interest initially from elite and then mass audiences. It was well embedded in traditional visual arts by the 20th century with characteristically simple lines, stylized features, and they tended to express humorous satire and a dose of spiritual optimism. After World War II, *manga* got an additional boost from the West, inspired from American comics, like *Superman.*

There are many people whose interest in Japanese culture and language started after exposure to *manga* or *anime.* These days, there are even hugely popular conventions organized the world over—drawing passionate fans for a period of several days, to network with like-minded aficionados as well as show their passion and dedication.

Fans can also gather to buy merchandise and try "cosplay," a term derived from "costume play" which involves fans dressing up as (and impersonating) their favorite character for the day. Cosplay is not restricted to *anime* having also crossed over to Western comics, cartoon series, and even Hollywood movies and video games.

Many anime contain characters described as *otaku,* which in English is often conveyed as nerd, geek or fanboy. The notion of a character having the traits of an *otaku* is found in many cultures, although not every language has a precise name for it. In Japan, it's been used, since the 1980s, to refer to people who are passionate about anime, *manga,* and videogames. Etymologically, the word's origins lie in the polite form of the second-person pronoun meaning "your home" with connotations of having an obsessive interest in something—an all-consuming passion at the expense of everything else. It can even extend to an obsessive interest in a variety of topics, be they trains, aerospace, or the military. This exclusion of the outside world and sociality is compatible, or so some social psychologists may argue, with the total withdrawal associated with *hikikomori*: a tribe of regressive young people who never emerge from home, unable to socially either "fit in" or "mature." But the implied immaturity and stunted socialization might not be radically different from the behavior of the Showa Emperor who, on a visit to America, put Disneyland first on his social itinerary.

So, there is a wider pattern here that finds expression in several facets of the culture. The embrace of the common or the diminutive as opposed to the "grand vision thing" (to borrow from the late George H.W. Bush) implies a degree of stunted social development even as it connotes intimacy and finding refuge in the familiar. The common Japanese suffix *ko* for women's names is quite literally translated as "little one" much like the use of *-akis, -itsa, -oulis, -oula* in the Greek language. *Giorgos* becomes *Giorgakis, Anna* becomes *Annoula* and so on. Modern Greek is replete with diminutives well beyond forenames: a coffee is routinely referred to as *cafedaki,* a cat is *gatoula* while wine becomes *krasaki,* mostly denoting affection or intimacy. So, the use of the diminutive can be seen as a semantic universal, typically to underscore intimacy and informality, but in the Japanese context it is often associated with immersion in one's "child self" much as the *otaku* phenomenon represents a child-like fixation with a single pursuit at the exclusion of all others.

The Japanese *ningyō* (doll) obsession may also be a variant of this proclivity for the diminutive and reversion to a child state. *Hinamatsuri* on March 3rd every year is devoted to the display of (often very expensive) miniaturized ornamental dolls (*hina ningyō,* 雛人形) brought out for display by adults, on red-cloth covered platforms. It is ostensibly focused on families with young daughters but the tradition is enthusiastically embraced by all age groups.

Galbraith (2014) extensively researched the *otaku* phenomenon in his *Otaku Encyclopedia* in which he explains some the glaring downsides of the term: "People are taking individual play and consumptive pleasure beyond acceptable limits, up to the point of upsetting their social functioning." He later adds that the definition applies to "People who are perceived to let hobbies get in the way of taking on "adult" roles and responsibilities at work and home," yet some might argue that young Japanese corporate employees working unpaid overtime until 9 P.M. may also suffer from atrophied social skills. While the term has generally carried negative connotations, many self-described *otaku* now self-identify with it with great pride! This might suggest that those *otaku* addicted to video games are not so different from the mainstream culture in terms of social detachment and emotional maladjustments.

Chapter 5

The Social Dark Side

Japan's miraculous recovery following the widespread destruction of WWII was followed by a period of relative affluence and growth. When you are in survival mode, your natural tendency is to do everything necessary to make ends meet. As you move up on the pyramid postulated by Maslow's hierarchy of needs, your pursuits and goals become more social and personal fulfillment driven. It's no surprise then that Japan's younger generation has placed more emphasis on meaning and fulfillment in the kinds of jobs they seek. Time and again, research on employee motivation and engagement has shown that for most people a critical ingredient of engagement is finding meaning in one's work while maintaining positive relationships. This is a universal phenomenon and Japan is no different. It is just that in Japan some emergent work arrangements, which are transient (and often missing the link to long-term career objectives or purpose), contrast strongly with the more stable, long-term and purposefully chosen careers of the past. The traditional expectation of lifelong employment has gone by the wayside with the emergence of *furiita* (フリータ ー), part-timers who are employed in the increasingly common gig-economy. At the same time, the Japanese labor market has seen the emergence of jobs labelled "The 3K: *kitanai* (dirty), *kiken* (dangerous), and *kitsui* (demeaning)." And then there are the "NEET's" or "nuclear gypsies": temp workers who do the least desirable work in the nuclear power industry (McCurry, 2011).

Karōshi: Death Through Overwork

And if you don't die by being exposed to nuclear waste, you should know that the Japanese coined the word *karōshi*, which refers to pathologically high levels of stress from overwork, in many documented cases leading to death. That's a bit more than being a workaholic, in any language. But it may well be embraced socially as the ultimate sacrifice to the group, and hence resistant to any efforts to impose legal restrictions upon unpaid overtime in the interest of preserving collective duty over the selfishness implied in the notion of "free" time.

Death from overwork is a serious and enduring problem in Japan. There are many examples of such deaths, which led to considerable soul-searching and, in some cases, law suits. Advertising giant Dentsu's gruelling workplace culture had been intensely scrutinized after one of the agency's young employees Matsuri Takahashi committed suicide in 2015. This led to the resignation of the CEO, Tadashi Ishii, in 2016. By taking responsibility for the incident, he ensured at least partial closure to what had begun to snowball into a PR disaster.

Karōshi is one of the many pathologies afflicting Japan to which I've given the general description of the "social dark side." Indeed, subsumed within this heading are special social groups and social phenomena that add to the country's intriguing mix:

The "Water Trade"

The euphemism water trade (*mizu shōbai*) has been used to refer to Japan's expansive nightlife entertainment industry, replete with brothels, nightclubs, "hostesses," and the iconic *geisha* and their apprentices, the *maiko*.

◇◇◇

Two maiko performing in Gion.
(Photo by Jon Rawlinson, Wikimedia Commons – CC BY 2.0)

Geisha find their roots in female entertainers of the 7th century and the *shirabyōshi* who appeared in the early 13th century. They were performing for the nobility, and some even became concubines to the emperor. In the late 16th century, the first pleasure quarters were built and typically had surrounding walls. Like so many aspects of Japanese culture, these quarters were modelled after those of China's Ming Dynasty. After relocation in the mid-1600s, they became known as *shimabara* (after a fortress in Kyushu).

Arthur Golden's 1998 novel, *Memoirs of a Geisha*, is the story of Nitta Sayuri and her life as a *geisha*. It begins in a poor fishing village in 1929 when a nine-year-old girl with unusual blue-gray eyes is taken from her home and sold into a famous *geisha* house. There she learns the arts of the *geisha*: singing, dancing, and playing traditional instruments. They wore beautiful silk *kimono* and elaborate makeup, which may strike a Westerner as rather quaint if not grotesque.

Some in the West interpret the word *geisha* as the equivalent of a prostitute, but the nuance conveyed by "courtesan" is a lot closer to the historical reality, for it involves accompanying entertainment skills, including perhaps the samisen or dancing. The word *geisha* is literally composed of two *kanji* meaning "art" plus "person" or "doer." Even though popular perceptions in the West saw *geisha* as sophisticated prostitutes, this does not reflect their actual role as artistic entertainers. They were highly proficient in singing, dancing and playing traditional music instruments, to entertain important guests—nothing more. Cultural performance is not strictly separated from potential physical performance as certain American film producers of late have affirmed. Business and pleasure have never been separable with ease in the country as company-sponsored drinking sessions after work (where business decisions continue) clearly illustrate. Over time, that distinction may have got rather blurred as rich men became lifelong patrons (or *danna*) for some *geisha*—who became more akin to a long-time second wife or mistress.

So, typically *geisha* and *maiko* were distinct from traditional sex traders, the so-called *oiran*. These high-class escorts or courtesans are a permanent fixture of Japanese cities" night entertainment districts along with the numerous "hostesses" who work in night clubs and are there to keep you company, make conversation, and often share a drink. Again, in typical Japanese fashion, the lines may be rather blurred with some overlap between them, which requires high-context discernment. Like the distinction in France between an *appellation d'origine contrôlée* 3rd growth St. Julien and an IGP (formerly *Vin du Pays*) wine, there is a cultivated difference in taste (and probably price) lost on the novice to both experiences replete with disappointments and surprising delights. One more expensive wine is to be "laid down" for the future; the other is to be consumed now, perhaps literally as a "screw cap." Delicacy is different from quaffing, but it carries the connotation of taste, appreciation of skills, and discretion. This last skill, discretion, was on display two decades ago when a "hostess" revealed to a tabloid publication that she was having an affair with a cabinet minister who had been rather *ketchi* (cheap) and was in arrears with his monthly allowance. Several people commented that a real *geisha* would have never complained publicly and that the cabinet member had proved his parsimony by getting exactly what he was paying for: an amateur bar girl. He resigned shortly thereafter.

Organized Crime

Japan's version of mafia or a crime family (*yakuza*) has its origins in the country's medieval past. The word *yakuza* originally referred to a gang member, but today it is also used for Japanese organized crime as a whole. A synonym, *bōryokudan*, is quite derogatory and refers to degenerate, tattoo-coated, violent gangsters with no sense of tradition or honor—far from the idealized way in which *yakuza* see themselves, which is more like modern-day "philanthropists."

◇◇◇

Tattooed yakuza members.
(Photo by Jorge, Wikimedia Commons – CC BY 2.0)

The *yakuza*'s most direct ancestors are groups of quasi-legal businessmen from the 18th century who gambled or peddled goods on the streets of large cities. Known as *bakuto* and *tekiya* respectively, these gamblers and peddlers lend their names to some *yakuza* clans today. These groups gradually organized themselves into gangs known as families or clans, which had formal hierarchies and rules (akin to the mafia). Many *yakuza* are also said to belong to the *burakumin* class, descendants of outcasts and their socially "tainted" occupations such as undertakers, executioners, butchers, and leather workers—a remnant of the highly hierarchical feudal era that is a precursor to the widespread prejudice that still exists in Japan.

In the late 19th century, the *yakuza* became associated with nationalist and militaristic ideologies. Gangs cultivated alliances with politicians who in turn used them to assassinate opponents, strong-arm individuals or groups, and for all kinds of extortionary or bullying tactics. The disorder of post-World-War-II Japan was fertile ground for the *yakuza*, providing them an even stronger economic clout than before (Kaplan et al., 2012).

While the government and the press call the *yakuza* "violent groups," the gangs predictably use favorable (and one could say "flowery") descriptions of themselves. "Chivalrous organizations" is one such self-descriptor, alluding to imagery associated with modern-day Robin Hoods rather than outright criminals. In fact, that may have been reinforced among some Japanese in the aftermath of the highly destructive Kobe earthquake in 1995. It was widely reported at the time that the disaster relief provided by organized yakuza groups was faster and more efficient than that provided by the government, helping them earn considerable social credit in the process.

Coping With The Emotional Deficit

Social clumsiness is a pervasive problem in Japan, particularly in urban areas where most young people feel ill at ease around other people. In part, this is the reason for the phenomenon of *hikikomori*, which refers to young people staying at their family home beyond the age when this is regarded as normal. Rather than go out, they prefer the comfort of their own home and engaging in compulsive "loner" pursuits such as playing video games and surfing the internet. This has even led to many people spurning real relationships (including sex) preferring the predictability and simplicity of the cyberspace—an environment where their actions have no consequences and where they can experiment with alternative versions of self. Here, they can try new identities or "new selves" of sorts without the "risk" of social judgment that comes with it. A survey conducted by the Japanese National Institute of Population and Social Security Research in 2011 found that nearly two of three unmarried men and one in two unmarried women aged 18–34 were not in any kind of romantic relationship. Another survey by the Japan Family Planning Association (JFPA) found that 45% of women aged 16–24 "were not interested in or despised sexual contact." By replacing real intimacy with a comfortable cocoon of make-believe, virtual gratification is a phenomenon that is perhaps not confined to Japanese society (even though I would argue that the degree to which it exists is especially high). Instant gratification without any of the complexities of real relationships is something that seems to afflict millenials the world over albeit not to the same degree. This generation is gradually losing the ability to deal with real people, preferring the predictability and "fix" of the virtual. What MIT's Sherry Turkle refers to as "disintegration of self" can be seen as a defense mechanism for narcissistic and one could say impoverished personalities.

What we give up in terms of compassion, empathy, and, more generally, social sensitivity is perhaps of great significance to our cultural resilience. I have often wondered what societies such as Japan's give up when they amplify the already strong biological drive to succeed and defeat others (shaped through tens of thousands of years of evolution) and allow it to morph into narcissism driven by excessive stress on achievement and competition—in which case it may be regarded as pathological.

Looked at more prosaically, the feelings of estrangement and social clumsiness among a sizeable segment of the population have created countless business opportunities. They say that money can't buy you love, but in Japan, you can buy the appearance of love through simulation and play-acting. Take a company called "Family Romance" that provides professional actors to fill any role in a client's personal life. Business has been booming, with the number of staff growing rapidly: they employ hundreds of "actors," ranging from young children to the elderly, and provide a surrogate for almost any conceivable social or private situation. They can be your best friend, husband, father, or even a mourner at your funeral.

'Family Romance" owner Yuichi Ishii helps people cope with any perceived deficiencies in their lives with human interaction that can be purchased on demand. In an increasingly isolated society, Family Romance's CEO predicts the rapid growth of his and similar businesses (Morin, 2017). In fact, a fairly recent variant of this trend—again fueled by pervasive feelings of social isolation—is the practice of hiring a "middle-aged man" to play-act as a relative, family friend or business associate. An *ossan* or *ojisan* may come in handy if you just need someone to consult (being a good listener is probably the most important trait) or even impersonate your father, uncle, or boss at a wedding or important reception. He'll even do a speech for you if asked! All you need to do is visit the company's website and follow a fairly easy process:

- Choose among available "ossan" in your area
- Provide your information
- Go to "check out" where you key-in your credit card details

- Stipulate arrangements on where/when to meet and the detailed requirements of the "rental."

Perhaps a largely unintended consequence of this trend is that it has somehow helped change the imagery associated with the word "ossan." Traditionally, "old man" has had rather negative connotations (in the "dirty old man" sense) but that is now changing in the minds of most people, especially the young.

Divorce Ceremonies

Another interesting entrepreneurial niche is that of divorce planners who offer meticulous and often elaborate planning arrangements to couples who decide to "untie the knot." Regarded as socially unacceptable for centuries, divorce is becoming much more common with roughly one in three couples eventually going their separate ways. This rate is still not alarming by international standards but certainly represents a major change over perceptions and practices just a few decades ago when couples persevered in dysfunctional relationships no matter what. So, as more couples opt to end their marriage vows, some astute entrepreneurs have come up with the idea of a divorce ceremony (*rikon shiki*) where attendees come to witness the end of a relationship—just as they did when the wedding ceremony marked its beginning. Whoever is chosen to speak on behalf of the couple typically starts his or her speech with the rather absurd *rikon omedeto gozaimasu* ("congratulations on your divorce"). Then again, if this is marking a rite of passage that is aimed at soothing a future (non-committal) relationship and a new life, the word congratulations may not be that inappropriate.

Some rites involved in the ceremony may involve the smashing of wedding rings with both former partners wielding a hammer. If the relationship had involved a go-between or matchmaker (*nakōdo*) he or she may also be present, acknowledging the failure of their "arrangement." Presumably, this is a time when the

Japanese expression for "I'm sorry" (*sumimasen,* denoting regret yet literally meaning "we aren't finished yet") adds a perplexing twist to the intended nuance.

Some may see the ritualization of this new rite of passage as simply evidence of commercial acumen on the part of some who have managed to turn the rising divorce rates into a major revenue generating opportunity. But it may also represent something a bit more nuanced, reflecting a deeply ingrained need for reaching finality, a "marker" of sorts for the end of an important relationship just as there was for the beginning. Rituals may represent ways of relieving anxiety or of providing a sense of control over life circumstances, ameliorating the trauma associated with rupture or dissent.

Indeed, many life events have tended to be "ritualized" in Japanese culture, just as the engagement ceremony had morphed into prescribed protocols that involve expensive diamond rings, the price of which represents specific multiples of the prospective groom's salary. This formulaic approach was a welcome boon for De Beers and other diamond manufacturers as it created a huge new industry where none had traditionally existed!

Love Hotels

Many first-time visitors to Japan may mistake the existence of thousands of "love hotels" (or short-stay hotels) where customers can pay for a room, by the hour, with an appropriate ambience, as a sign of a higher than usual frolicking. One may justifiably wonder why infidelity seems to be so pervasive in a country in which loyalty is so highly valued. It turns out that the explanation has less to do with infidelity and more to do with the lack of privacy in most households. Cramped conditions drive couples (married or otherwise) to seek privacy for a few hours in districts, which offer a wide range of themed choices with typically *kitsch* decors. The tens of thousands of love hotels have in fact fallen on hard times

◇◇◇

Love Hotel in Kabukichō, Tokyo.
(Photo by Chris 73, Wikimedia Commons – CC BY-SA 3.0)

in light of the rise in voluntary or involuntary celibacy, to a certain extent driven by the replacement of real intimacy with all forms of cybersex. The preference for the virtual at the expense of the real yet more messy experience is becoming a real concern, especially in a country facing demographic decline. For now, however, love hotels are a prominent feature of the urban fabric and will remain so in the foreseeable future.

In case you just happen to wander into such a district by chance, there are obvious giveaways: gaudy themes with heart symbols and cupids, and, if you venture to go inside, you'll find rotating beds, ceiling mirrors, and jacuzzis to indulge in. As for colors, pink seems to predominate!

When a young foreign lady friend of mine tried to book her Canadian parents into a love hotel by mistake, the receptionist first wondered what kind of kinkiness drove the young one into the company of an older couple. The situation became even weirder (and perhaps more hilarious) when she asked for a room for several days, rather than the customary few hours! Love hotels often discourage the patronage of singles for fear of depressed individuals vulnerable to suicide, which has been known to tarnish the reputation of an institution dedicated to pleasure and bringing people together.

Cuddle Cafés

Another way in which people try to cope with anomie is by using *soineya* or "cuddle cafés." If you're single (but averse to visiting brothels or massage parlors), before you resign yourself to another lonely night, you may stop by a *soineya*, where clients can pay to sleep in the arms of an attractive girl—with no strings attached. The first *soineya* opened in 2012 in Tokyo's Akihabara electronics district, home of *otaku* culture.

What's on the "cuddle café" menu? Options start with a 20-minute nap and range up to 10 hours, or a very full night's rest. In addition to napping, clients can order other delights like "Girl pats customer on the back" or "Girl sleeps with head on customer's lap" (Simonitch, 2012).

It's perhaps worth expanding on another coping mechanism for anomie, namely the *maid cafés* that also sprung up in Akihabara in the early 2000s. Trying to capitalize on the fascination with *manga* and *anime*, the cafés allowed the acting out of *anime* fantasies among the hordes of *otaku*, creating a kind of "fantasy land" (not the Disney variety). The girls who work here (remember, there are no male maids around) dress in short frilly dresses, knee socks, and cat ears, an attire that is most familiar to *manga aficionados*.

There are no windows in maid cafés and no photos are allowed. Customers are expressly cautioned not to touch the maids, or ask for their phone numbers, a restriction that duplicates what was initially practiced at Playboy Bunny Clubs in the US: a prohibition that of course increases desire. And it's generally akin to the Playboy venue, not seedy or gaudy. Guys can even bring their girlfriends along, while business colleagues may visit on their lunch breaks. Yet these oddities have a certain kind of logic, as they seemingly offset stunted personality development and inadequate socialization.

The Pachinko Parlor Obsession

These ubiquitous pinball-like gaming parlors are a cacophonous expression of anomie and social maladjustment if there ever was one. *Pachinko*, played with boxes of steel balls that bang together incessantly, is a national obsession as well as being an extremely profitable business.

By some estimates, the *pachinko* industry generates 4% of Japanese GDP, or more than the gaming/gambling industries

◇◇◇

Pachinko parlor, Tokyo.
(Photo by Michael Maggs, Wikimedia Commons – CC BY-SA 3.0)

of Las Vegas and Macau combined. Winners are often required to exit the parlor to claim their winnings at a separate window on a nearby side street (Hincks, 2017). Like *karaoke*, there is a kind of emptiness at the core of this peculiar entertainment venue insofar as one never directly claims his winnings on the spot, but must redeem it for say, a ham, elsewhere from an issued "chit." There is always a mediator, just as is the case with the clerk behind the curtain collecting your bill at a love hotel. This occurs in an environment often permeated with the "surround-sound" of martial music as one plays the games derived from pinball, played by American (military) occupiers after World War II. Often the owners of the pachinko salons are shadowy figures, disguising their actual ownership behind a plethora of shell companies. When our neighborhood community association complained of the noise and engaged an attorney in preparation for a lawsuit against plans to establish an outlet, the lawyer filed a sequence of "discovery" applications, ultimately successful, in order to locate a potential singular defendant. It is an apt metaphor for the "layered" (*nemawashi*) environment pervading Japanese everyday life.

Personally, I could never understand how intelligent people can sit in such noisy, smoky parlors, mechanistically playing away at a completely meaningless pursuit (unless you are one of those so adept that you can make a quick profit). Of course, aspiring philosophers may see "Zen-like" qualities in playing the game, though to me the very act of frequenting these places is an expression of serious social dysfunction. I once went into one while I was living in Kyoto, but left minutes later shaking my head in disbelief after seeing a woman holding an infant in her arm while playing with the other. Someone should have called social services perhaps? Or is it possible that pachinko with its large panel screen and ball steered by a "joystick" for hours on end was a precursor of the video game, so successfully marketed by Nintendo and others?

There are more aspects to the social underbelly than the examples provided above but this analysis was meant to illuminate aspects of psychological maladjustment, rather than treat the subject in an exhaustive manner.

Superstition

I've already touched upon uncertainty avoidance in our discussion of Hofstede's cultural dimensions. While this finds expression in positive and much-needed contingency plans to mitigate natural disasters, it is also evident in less rational domains such as superstition.

Take inauspicious numbers for example: Like unlucky 13 in the West, the number 4 or *shi* in Japan is regarded as ill-fated as it is pronounced "death" even though the *kanji* or ideogram is different. The number 9 is similarly avoided as it denotes suffering (again, a matter of identical pronunciation).

Numerology is also the basis for *rokuyō* , the lucky and unlucky days of the Japanese calendar. It affects weddings, funerals, baby booms, and even starting a new business. When moving house, you may choose to move on a day regarded as auspicious in which case you will most probably pay a premium. If you want a bargain, go for an inauspicious day (the worst possible one, if you can choose).

Astrology and divination of all kinds are a part of life for a significant number of Japanese. House divination (or *ecomancy,* the term I used during my graduate studies to describe the practice) is the codification of certain common-sense rules related to the layout of houses. As I've noted previously, there are auspicious layouts and orientations of houses and gardens, based on the ancient Chinese practice of feng-shui or geomancy. *Kasō* (or house divination, a variant of Chinese *feng-shui*) was a practice that governed (and still does in some cases) the siting and layout of houses in Japan.

For those readers who have experienced sumo wrestling, they have undoubtedly witnessed the wrestlers' tossing of handfuls of salt to "purify" the fighting ring. You can even find temples not far outside Tokyo where you can literally wash and blow dry your paper money: your cash is expected to increase as a result.

Suicide and its Broad Acceptance

Suicide is a hugely sensitive and complex issue with a multitude of underlying causes, one of the most serious of which is acute mental distress. In many cases this is a manifestation of various forms of mental illness such as acute anxiety, depression, and the like. Undoubtedly, its clinical variants which some researchers believe are attributable to chemical imbalance (lower than normal levels of neurotransmitters) are a major cause of suicide but so are social factors such as deep stress and trauma (sexual abuse, bullying, and the like) or highly stressful life events (loss of job, divorce, failing in school). The latest neuroscience research, in fact, suggests that mental disorders can have a biological cause but as with many physical illnesses, they can also have a strong emotional component. Be that as it may, suicide is the ultimate response to deep emotional pain—a desperate flight from reality—and Japanese society's view on it has evolved considerably from the days of ritual *seppuku*. The suicide rate in Japan has always been high per capita, for a time second only to Hungary (even though the latest OECD statistics place Japan 5th and Hungary 6th). It tends to be higher among males, typically after some heartbreak: a divorce, loss of a job, financial difficulties, and the like, perceived as shameful. These "rejections" can seem somewhat trivial to Westerners. I knew an academic who had failed a student on some exam during the year only to have the sobbing twenty-two-year-old at his office door, claiming that the mid-term test was "her whole life." He correctly drew her attention to the difference between tests and life: though life may be a test, tests are seldom all of life.

Some commentators have noted that the cultural tolerance for suicide lies in the acceptance of it morally among large segments of a population. Of course, *seppuku* or *harakiri* has always had a heroic connotation, no doubt fostered by the extensive narratives around *bushidō* culture and *samurai*. The ritual act of disembowelment to avoid falling into the hands of the enemy is in no way analogous to modern suicide but the lack of a religious sanction against the practice is quite notable. So is its conflation with "weakness" in modern times, which perhaps accounts for its under-reporting. If Ruth Benedict's distinction in *The Chrysanthemum and the Sword*—that Japan is a "shame" culture rather than a "guilt" culture—is apposite, then the "place" of suicide in the society may owe something to an antecedent militaristic code of honor rather than a court or legal system determining a prescribed "schedule" of punishments for specific crimes. This would of course not be incompatible with *ijime* ("bullying") or other forms of scape-goating in cultures with a similar heritage. John Lukacs is not the only historian to have reminded us that when the Third Reich collapsed, as many as 10,000 Germans committed suicide, not all of them Nazis (*The New York Times International Edition*, May 10, 2019, p.2), but descendants nonetheless of a Junker code of honor sharing certain characteristics with the *butoh* (the dance of death and disease) of its Axis ally in World War II.

Interestingly, as the suicide rate in Japan has seen a decrease, the corresponding rate in the US now approaches epidemic proportions, and this does not include opioid addiction, a rather derivative form of self-destruction.

Chapter 6

Business

My initial seven years as a resident in Japan were mostly spent in Kyoto in a comfortable academic cocoon familiar to students and academics the world over. Although the pressure to get good grades and publish academic papers was there, as I moved to doctoral and then postdoc status, I began to realize that this rather complacent setting stood in stark contrast to the bustling business worlds of Tokyo, Osaka, and the automotive heartland, Nagoya. I didn't have the opportunity to witness firsthand Japan's business culture until I received a call from the Foreign Student Affairs office at Kyoto University, asking if I was interested in talking to a Japanese shipping company about some interpreting work they needed. I agreed to their terms and later devoted a couple of days to being involved in talks with a Greek delegation of ship owners.

At first, the two sides merely talked past each other. The Greeks were eager to get into the details of a possible deal (buying a couple of ships to complement their fleet), while the Japanese showed little desire to discuss specifics. Rather, they wanted to get to know the visitors and talk about the general principles of any deal before getting into any meaningful detail. The Greek communication was to the point and explicit; the Japanese were much more nuanced and, one could say, evasive. It took a while, especially after a couple of lunches and dinners—where alcohol flowed freely—for the Japanese to begin discussing substantive matters.

During these discussions, I realized what many foreign companies come to realize after initially banging their heads against the proverbial Japanese wall:

- Initial meetings are to establish rapport and not jump into detail.
- The person who spoke most on the Japanese side (typically the one whose command of English was passable) was in fact not a decision-maker. The ones who mattered typically stayed silent, giving clear cues to their team, but staying out of direct exchanges. Whereas we in the West tend to mistake silence for weakness or lack of knowledge (having nothing to say is somehow viewed as a deficiency), the Japanese see silence and reserve as leadership traits. They do not equate the one who talks a lot (or well) for someone who has clout. In fact, they view it as the initial warmup!
- Decisions aren't made at meetings, but by long consensus-building sessions of *"nemawashi"*— several rounds of "pre-meetings" before the official meeting where a decision is announced, not made. The metaphor draws on a gardening practice where a plant's roots are prepped before the plant is re-potted.

This all-important step of consensus-building within the organization wasn't apparent to either me or the Greek visitors until it was explained to me over dinner by a Japanese team member.

After a few cups of *saké* he gave me some invaluable pointers on how these interactions usually play out. In fact, one who mistakes this process for inefficiency misses an important point: Spending time building consensus enables the Japanese to move much faster from there on!

To illustrate the difference in business cultures, a Japanese friend once told me:

"Americans send a couple of people to a meeting to tell you everything they believe you need to know. The Japanese send more than 10 people to the same meeting—to learn everything you know." To the Japanese, meetings are primarily aimed at getting to know you and your company. *Nemawashi* normally follows, when ideas are discussed and decisions finally made.

An then, of course, is the initial business card exchange ritual. It's a must when you first meet a Japanese businessman or businesswoman. The card is given and received with both hands, and not just placed (or, God forbid, thrown) on the table—a major no-no. Apart from the fact that it signifies pride in representing the company, it provides critical cues for what kind of language to use (and how deep to bow!), depending on the status of the person you're exchanging cards with.

The language aspect is not as vital when meeting foreigners (but of utmost importance when the Japanese themselves meet), but the unspoken social interaction cues still apply: deference shown to those of higher rank, choosing who to look at when making a toast, to whom to first bow, etc. Where one sits is also important: At dinner, the most senior person typically sits farthest from the door, while the most junior sits closest. Becoming adept at such social cues requires some time for a foreigner but comes quite naturally to a Japanese. The more time I spent in Japan, the more natural these behaviors seemed to me, becoming an automatic response to predictable situations.

Workplace Attitudes and Behavior

One of the dynamics behind workplace behavior is the tradition of lifetime employment. It has been part of the social contract; the certainty around one's future and the loyalty the company receives in return. I especially appreciated this when I ran Synovate's global solutions and visited Japan to review our operations and visit clients. The notion that once you have a job in a company, you stay there for life, is a glue that binds life together and often drives performance. I visited "family" in this sense as my colleagues were prone to provide full support in my every effort. Indeed, the reciprocity in such relationships is clear: The company offers security and a wide range of perks in return for loyalty and extra effort. In organizational psychology, we often refer to this as the psychological contract: the implicit or unwritten aspects of the employment relationship—what we are prepared to do for the company and what we want back in return. This is perhaps a defining characteristic of what some have termed the "community company," one that aligns long-term security with a commonality of purpose (Inagami, Whittaker, 2005).

Typically, the lifetime employment journey starts with *shūshoku katsudō*, the mass job hunting ritual that for most young people culminates with getting hired at a corporation in April, the beginning of the fiscal year. The job hunt starts early (while still at university, as early as the junior year) and is marked by attending career seminars or corporate "get to know us" job fairs at campuses. So systematized is the system that *Keidanren* (the Japan Business Federation) set a schedule every year for recruiting activity by its members. This mass hiring round has come under considerable criticism leading *Keidanren* to issue revised guidelines that reflect both the labor shortage and the need for diversity. Indeed, many companies now offer jobs year-round, not just in spring. So, change is afoot not only as regards job security but the ways in which one joins that one and only employer—and how lasting that relationship is expected to be.

A similar idea, but adapted to the consumer, is the effort to maintain mutually beneficial long-term loyalty. Notably, the adaptation of the *kaisūken* ("coupon ticket") system initially introduced by Japan Railways for frequent travelers. Unlike America (with seasonal mark-up and mark-downs deceptively deemed "Clearance Sales") or the Singapore use of the "Lucky Sticker" (a draw for prizes), the Japanese deploy cards stamped or points awarded for each purchase that can be accumulated over time (they never expire). The barber shop gives a ticket with blank spaces for dates to be filled in. After ten have been punched, the customer gets a free haircut. The more often you get groomed, the cheaper it becomes! It is in the mutual interest of both to maintain the card, as opposed to migrating to the competition, induced by a lower price and close familiarity. The "frequency discount" model was of course adopted by airline loyalty and other programs in the West, but a couple of decades later. One possible predecessor in Japan was the so-called "bottle keep" bar, where one purchased a bottle of whiskey (it can be cognac but that is much less common) but on which one's name was hung. The "owner" then had an incentive to return to the same establishment where he paid only a "service charge" to a hostess for pouring and mixing his *mizuwari* ("whiskey cut with water"). In the process, a bar becomes a social club with a more devoted following than the "lonely drunk" model celebrated in Billy Joel's "Piano Man."

It seems to me that this innovation might be an instance of a horizontal "loyalty" system as opposed to the much stronger and durable vertical system that binds employees and companies, as a family.

Office Etiquette

Another characteristic of Japanese employment practice that is gradually changing is the pressure to conform. Traditionally this was relentless and was evident by the army of salarymen, typically dressed in business attire and going about their daily duties. But old habits die hard. Employees are often reluctant to leave work until the boss does first (irrespective of family-related "distractions") and this is not likely to change any time soon. In fact, a story circulates of a certain foreign employee working in a large corporation in Tokyo. Like all the Japanese staff, he was expected to stay until the boss left in the evening. The boss happened to be even more diligent (or slower) than most, so the foreigner kept a bottle of bourbon in his desk, which he routinely slipped into his coffee cup on tedious late nights.

From these early experiences, many of the same themes played out in multiple business situations, including those where my organization was the client and vice-versa. In fact, when you deal with Japanese companies as suppliers, you can guarantee that what they promise will be delivered! In all my years doing business with Japanese, I don't recall a single case where an agreed deliverable wasn't submitted on time (a routine occurrence in many parts of the world where excuses come as naturally as a morning greeting). This feature of Japanese logistics continually amazes visitors, accustomed to delayed deliveries. On arrival at any major airport in Japan with very heavy baggage, logistics companies await after customs clearance to pick up your 20 kg. bag and deliver it to a hotel room or domicile door for about 2,000 yen ($22), nationwide. You check a box for the time of nationwide delivery the following day (i.e., 8–10 ; 10–12; 12–2; 2–4; 4–6). We have used the service over a dozen times: your heavy bag and its dirty clothes and gifts are never late. On-time delivery is an industry.

In fact, in most meetings related to scoping work to be done, and mutual commitments, the insistence on tackling every seemingly minor detail seems "over the top" to many non-Japanese. Yet, the understanding that "the devil is in the detail" drives much of the pre-planning, planning, and implementation of any engagement involving the Japanese. As they look for long-term relationships, Japanese companies may initially award a "test" project. This is followed by a larger assignment if all goes well. It's wise to make sure that the first small project is executed flawlessly if you truly want to make inroads into their business ecosystem.

Earlier in this chapter, I already recounted the case of a Japanese acquaintance living in London whose job was to report back to his head office (a major department store) on the activities of high-end UK department stores. An example of the age-old practice of "adopt, adapt, and become adept"? Of course, competitive intelligence isn't unique to Japanese firms, but I doubt UK department stores go to the expense of sending full-time "scouts" to other countries to monitor best practices.

When discussing Japan's business environment these also form an important part of the overall context.

Capsule Hotels

You may be familiar with the *sarariman*—the blue-suited drones who throng Japanese business districts. He (as he is typically male) often stays out late, particularly to entertain customers or associates, and when he misses the last train home around midnight, he heads for one of the capsule hotels that ring major train stations. Imagine coffin-sized beds stuck in a grid on a wall, with guests sleeping inside them. They're certainly not for the claustrophobic. On the other hand, think efficiency for the owner: a hotel of 1000 square feet, accommodating 30–50 heads a night. The alternative is to hail a taxi and spend at times more than 10,000 yen for the ride home. Especially in overcrowded Tokyo, with space at an exorbitant premium, such hotels are composed of individual sleeping units, complete with pajamas, a toothbrush, and the ubiquitous slippers. They offer a convenient, lower-priced alternative to riding home and then coming back again the next morning. Fresh for another bout at the office.

∞∞

Capsule Hotel, Osaka.
(Photo by J. Miers, Wikimedia Commons – CC BY-SA 1.0)

Kissatens: Extended Living Space

Many people use the ubiquitous *kissatens* (coffee shops) as extended living space, or to borrow from the founding CEO of Starbucks, a "third space" between work and home, combining elements of both. Big-city space is at a premium, so people often use coffee shops as their workspace or a place to socialize. There is no clear distinction between work and a variety of entertainments, be it part of a business or personal relationship. Rather than invite you to their home, many Japanese prefer to entertain outside which may also be seen as redistributing income to the less skilled. In the early '80s, there was a tax charged on all meals over 3,000 yen. In order to avoid the "luxury tax," people would eat and drink until just below the threshold, and then continue their drinking at another venue: an intriguing way of distributing patronage. It would certainly seem strange in the West to enter a coffee shop and see suited businessmen napping on the tables. But in Japan, the price of an expensive cup of coffee also buys a temporary office, and a generous supply of gossip mags or comic books, far enough from the "madding crowd."

I fondly remember my own experiences at Honyaradō, my favorite morning hangout during the early '80s. This is where I would enjoy my breakfast (or *morningu,* from the English "morning") often in the company of like-minded expats like Professor Jan Gordon (who wrote the Foreword to this book) and other close friends like Sidney Atkins, an American geographer doing post-graduate work at *Kyōdai.* For only slightly more than the cost of a cup of coffee you'd be offered a strong (and delicious) brew, freshly baked buttered toast, a hard-boiled egg, and a small salad. The perfect light breakfast before starting the day and sometimes, later in the day, a quiet space to write parts of my dissertation.

Gift Giving

Gift giving is an important ritual when dealing with the Japanese, particularly in business contexts. When visiting the head offices of a Japanese corporation, taking a gift is part of the expected protocol, with clear rules regarding to whom, how, and when it should be given. As with many aspects of their culture, it's ritualized with norms and practices that govern it, typical in a society where uncertainty avoidance is high. These practices typify reciprocity, generosity, and respect.

Consequently, there are prescribed rules on what kind of gift to give, how to give it, and when. Avoid surprising your host, while also not appearing to time your gift giving with an expectation of reciprocal action (although this is widely practiced). Let's look at the ritual in more detail.

- **What:** Gifts range from Grade A Kobe beef to perfectly shaped melons and even pricey pieces of art (such as paintings). Why is Kobe beef so dear? The cows are massaged, not allowed to move (much), fed high-quality food along with beer, and listen to classical music—all to create the world's finest (and most expensive) steak.
- **How:** Presentation is almost as important as the gift itself. The way it's wrapped needs to be immaculate and signify something of value and high quality.
- **To Whom:** Gifts are usually given to the most senior member of the team (if you're dealing with a group).
- **When:** The timing of gift giving is important and naturally should be auspicious.

Gift giving in Japan is enmeshed in a set of social conventions that almost prevent its "free" *giving*—in the sense of being a donation from the heart as opposed to a *transactional* practice. A gift valued at one-half the price of the gift one has received is customarily returned to the donor within a scheduled time period: seventy days for wedding gifts, one-hundred days for the *Koden*, monetary donations at funerals. Hence, it is difficult to give without receiving or to receive without giving. Like cross-held shares among companies, it is an extraordinary re-distribution system, insofar as it controls the largesse of those who might attempt to use the gift to gain control. As part of a web of pre-existent social relations, the symbolic exchange seems to nullify the materiality of the gift (Gordon, 1996). One result is a large supply of gifts, which often resist consumption.

Gift giving also manifests itself through the custom of *omiyage*: When you return to Japan from a business trip or vacation, your friends and colleagues may very well expect an *omiyage* or simple souvenir. These are token gifts, preferably conveying the flavor of the place you visited so it may be worth giving it some thought before opting for a tacky t-shirt with the word Bali engraved on it.

Continuous Improvement

Kaizen or "continuous improvement" is one of many Japanese business concepts, in some ways the opposite of *wabisabi* (explained briefly in "Chapter 2"). *Kaizen is* a new idea, coined only in 1986, and encapsulates a system that involves every employee, from upper management to the shop floor or the cleaning crew.

Everyone is continually encouraged to come up with small improvement suggestions. This is not a once-a-month or once-a-year activity. At companies such as Toyota, tens of suggestions per employee per year are captured, shared, and implemented on an ongoing basis. They're typically small improvements, not major changes but that is often the key point. So a Western employee should not be offended if his Japanese counterpart offers a suggestion for improvement. The philosophy of continuous improvement should not be seen as necessarily critical of the way things currently are. The point is that the current practice may be already superb, yet can still be improved! *Kaizen* would also encompass the vaunted "just in time" delivery system, a feature of Japanese production practices. The storage and maintenance of excess inventory is regarded as an unproductive use of both space and time; hence, a premium is placed upon synchronizing distribution and the efficient and timely deployment of disparate components needed at each stage of the final production chain.

Interlocking Business Groups

Keiretsu is a business network composed of manufacturers, supply chain partners, distributors, and financiers. This amounts to a loose conglomeration, often involving cross-shareholding. Members work closely together to ensure each other's success. Today's *keiretsu* include the horizontal model, which still has banks and trading companies at the top with significant control over each company's relevant activities. Shareholders replaced the families controlling the cartel as Japanese law allowed holding companies to supplement or altogether displace family ownership. Today, vertical integration is still a part of the larger horizontal structure so each of Japan's six car manufacturers belongs to one of the six *large keiretsus*. The same goes for Japan's major electronics companies.

Typical of a Japanese horizontal *keiretsu* is Mitsubishi with the Bank of Tokyo-Mitsubishi sitting at the top. Part of the core group is Mitsubishi Motors and Mitsubishi Trust and Banking, followed by Meiji Mutual Life Insurance Company, the provider of insurance services to all *keiretsu* members. As for distributing the goods around the world, that is the role of Mitsubishi Shōji, *the keiretsu's* trading company. They may seek new markets for *keiretsu* companies, help incorporate these companies in other nations, and sign contracts with other companies around the world to supply commodities used for Japanese industry. Often in the horizontal *keiretsu* arrangement, shares of the individual companies are cross-held, simultaneously mitigating risk, and, at least in the eyes of foreign competitors, effectively disguising quasi-monopolies.

A vertical *keiretsu* is a group of companies within the horizontal *keiretsu*. Perhaps the most famous of this arrangement is Toyota that depends on suppliers and manufacturers for parts, employees for production, real estate for dealerships, steel, plastics, and electronics suppliers for cars, in addition to wholesalers. All these ancillary companies operate within the vertical *keiretsu* of *Toyota*, but are still members of the larger horizontal *keiretsu*, albeit typically low on the organizational chart.

Without Toyota as the anchor company, these companies might not have a purpose for existence. The company is a major *keiretsu* member on account of its history and relationship to major horizontal members, dating back to the early years of the Meiji government when it became the first exporter of silk. The Japanese focus on societal relations, as well as cross-shareholdings, has allowed *keiretsus* to flourish since World War II. Failure to understand the *keiretsu* concept may cause problems in business relationships. Going for the most beneficial offer in most project tender situations is fair enough, but it should be grounded in an understanding of who within your *keiretsu* group may be able to offer the product/service you are looking for (Twomey, 2018).

Lifelong Employment

One source of Japanese business stability is the tradition of lifetime employment. The notion that once you have a job in a corporation you stay there for life creates a reciprocal relationship based on give and take. As a consequence, job mobility remains considerably lower in Japan than in other advanced economies (particularly the US). The practice of hiring straight from university, with the expectation that the employee will remain with the company until one retires, makes a lot of sense in periods of rapid growth. Once slower growth sets in, or there are macroeconomic imperatives for leaner operations, the model comes under strain. My own father-in-law, now deceased, was a loyal employee of Toshiba. Hired straight out of university, he rose through the ranks on account of sheer hard work and rising seniority. For this, he was rewarded with a variety of perks (such as holidays, albeit short, at company-owned compounds), plus security and stability for his family.

Lifelong employment also gives rise to the *madogiwa zoku* (literally "by the window tribe" or "by the window misfits"). Those who fail to rise in the ranks through promotion, usually due to limited capabilities, are "put out to pasture" and are discarded as misfits. They get a desk by the window and either have very little to do or carry out rather unimportant or "harmless" tasks. There is something primal or Darwinian in their plight, reminiscent of older lions who are cast out of their "pride" to live out their days on the fringes.

Consensus Building

Nemawashi is epitomized as several rounds of "pre-meetings" held ahead of the official meeting where a decision is announced (not necessarily made). It's contrasted with the Western idea of "top-down management" where upper management makes decisions that are then "forced" on the lower ranks. Obviously, decisions are made quickly, but implementation may languish—not typical in Japan. Of course, one could argue that we have similar processes in the West such as "consensus-building," "getting people on board," "obtaining buy-in," and "getting everyone on the same page." What many fail to realize is that *nemawashi* is actually a deep-seated way of doing things, not an ad-hoc response to a specific issue.

The Iron Triangle

The notion of *amakudari* ("descent from heavens") represents a deeply held traditional belief that the Japanese nation somehow has divine origins. In the business world, this is the term used to describe the practice of the hiring by corporations of former high-level bureaucrats (the metaphorical heavens being the highest echelons of the civil services) to ensure access to their extensive networks. The link between government and business is regarded as extremely important, especially in a society that places the utmost importance on personal relationships and loyalty. This gives rise to what has been referred to as the "iron triangle" between the civil service, politicians, and big business, through a web of mutually supportive relationships and interests. Despite efforts to curb the practice due to its obvious drawbacks (potential for collusion and corruption), it has proven to be very resilient.

The Quest for Perfection

I've already argued how the Japanese embrace imperfection and transience in nature, and how this pervades a certain aesthetic tradition. But in business, defining and executing standards of supreme quality proved to be a central plank for competitive differentiation. The obsessive search for perfection was seen as the key to establishing competitive differentiation (assuming that consumers were prepared to pay for the additional value). One TV drama, "Atelier," captures Japanese business practices and the world of high fashion in what has become one of the world's trendiest and hippest cities, Tokyo. Several themes reverberate in the series such as hierarchy and deference to the boss, the relentless pursuit of perfection and quality, and the Japanese devotion to customer-centricity. Again we see the insistence on "mastery," which comes from observing, sticking to clear instructions, and then following a long, arduous road to achieving true excellence.

In the world of high fashion, where establishments cater to discerning customers with deep pockets, this obsession translates to an air of sophistication, elegance, and exclusivity. Catering to the chosen few is a distinct position, but relentless attention to detail and effort need to always complement natural talent.

Avoiding Common Business Pitfalls

Being aware of Japanese business preferences and practices is vital to doing business with them. So is avoiding the frequent pitfalls not immediately apparent, that can make a big difference to the ultimate success or failure of ventures in the country. Some examples:

- Foreign HR professionals make the mistake of prioritizing English proficiency over competence and credibility (gravitas) among Japanese employees.
- The Japanese don't respond well to being under the management "thumb" of subsidiaries elsewhere in the region (i.e., Singapore, Hong Kong, or Shanghai). They'd prefer to interact directly with HQ in traditional centers like London, Paris, or New York.
- The failure to recognize that the Japanese approach to business is strictly long-term. It's much more about relationships than mere transactions.

I wrote earlier about the seeming contradictions noted in Ruth Benedict's view of Japanese culture. In fact, this is reflected in the business philosophy of one of the most successful corporations in the world, Toyota. In their book, *Extreme Toyota*, Osono et al. (2008) describe how six radical contradictions are woven into the Toyota way of working:

- Move gradually and take big leaps
- Cultivate frugality while spending huge sums
- Operate efficiently as well as redundantly
- Cultivate stability and a paranoid mindset
- Respect bureaucratic hierarchy and allow freedom to dissent
- Maintaining simplified and complex communication

To a Westerner, this may sound extremely confusing, but who are we to judge the operating credo of one of the most successful corporations in the world!

Accountability & Governance

Accountability and corporate governance are one of the topics that defy simple explanation. As with many facets of Japanese culture, it involves a blend of Western influence, yet persistent adherence to traditional values. The Anglo-American model of finance capitalism did exercise a certain pull on relevant legislation and managerial practices, yet was always going to be viewed as somewhat foreign to Japanese managerial philosophy. Fundamental in this discussion is the conception of the ultimate purpose of the firm (certainly not shareholder value it seems) and the role of outside board directors (which is more advisory than oversight and control). Whitakker and Deakin (2009) provide an in-depth analysis of this in their *Corporate Governance and Managerial Reform in Japan* (Oxford University Press). An excerpt:

> *The traditional or postwar model of Japanese corporate governance came under pressure in the "lost decade" of the 1990s and how a debate concerning corporate governance was launched in the early 2000s which led to a number of reforms, including legal encouragement for the appointment of independent directors and changes to takeover law in the aftermath of the Livedoor case in 2005... Japan's recent experience should not be seen either in terms of a delayed transition to the "global standard" on corporate governance or of simple resistance to the Anglo-American model. Instead there has been a managerial adaptation to, and reshaping of, the corporate governance reforms, which, paradoxically, has served to strengthen the core features of the Japanese "community firm."*

So, they conclude that even as Japanese executives pay more attention than before to shareholder value maximization, there has been no overwhelming support for it—one of the key tenets of finance capitalism that underpins Anglo-American corporate governance norms.

An interesting facet of any discussion on governance is the norms that surround what constitutes appropriate managerial behavior. I don't believe there has been a higher profile case of the breakdown in accountability than the fall of Carlos Ghosn, CEO of Nissan. The series of events that led to his imprisonment exemplify Japanese views on accountability and what constitutes acceptable behavior for a leader. He was stripped of his chairmanship and ended up in jail for hiding tens of millions of dollars in compensation, over a period of time, understating his real earnings by half. Humility was not one of Ghosn's strong points. He lobbied hard to get a compensation package that was far larger than any of his CEO peers in corporate Japan, while at the same time implementing strict cost-cutting across his own organization to increase margins. In fact, it is said that he wore his nickname "Le Cost Killer" as a badge of honor and felt no shame or contrition for earning four times more than Toyota's Chairman! In a culture that prizes humility, a sense of proportion, and team spirit, this behavior generated resentment! Without any more knowledge than what I have read in the press, the public response to Ghosn's actions is entirely understandable. In my experience, if one is going to dip into the company coffers, he must share the proceeds even symbolically. My exhibit A would be the *yakuza* practice of surrendering a representative of the group to the police after killing another syndicate boss. He may have had nothing to do with the crime, but serves the time (perhaps 2 years) after which he is promoted for his "group sacrifice" with the tacit concurrence of the police. That is "representative governance" *in extremis.*

A friend of mine once shared an experience he had at a Japanese university where he was a professor. He accidentally discovered that the remains of his book purchase account were used by other professors to host a party for their students. He had not known the money was in surplus but chose not to protest because they "shared" it with students. He concluded that no fuss was warranted! Turning now back to Ghosn, he seems to have committed the cardinal sin of using company money for his own private houses in Lebanon and Brazil. Neither Nissan nor Renault has a presence in Lebanon; hence it could not have been on business. Admittedly corporate governance is lax in Japan, but it is still rather statist and communitarian in spirit. Understating your income for tax purposes...well, that is definitely not very good, but in some cases may have been regarded as tolerable. How much time Ghosn will eventually spend in jail may be unclear but his name is mud—a selfish and self-serving executive, using Nissan's chartered Gulfstream to visit private houses in Brazil and Lebanon, as he apparently campaigned to be the President of Brazil! Normally, people of that wealth avoid serving time in jail. I don't recall Lehman Brothers" CEO, Fuld, being put behind bars for even a day. But ungenerous ostentation in Japan gets you in trouble every time. You give a nice donation (the *kōden*) at a funeral and within 45 days you are going to receive 1/2 of its value in the form of a gift certificate at a department store. You dare not give without receiving, nor receive without giving in this one.

Chapter 7

Language

Language is quintessentially a cultural expression. It is a medium for expressing and embodying the values, beliefs, and behavior of a given culture. This becomes particularly apparent when you learn Japanese: It's quite simple phonetically, yet complex when used in different social contexts. Simply put, there are three broad levels of the language, referred to collectively as honorifics or *keigo* (敬語):

- Polite: *Teineigo* (丁寧語)
- Respectful: *Sonkeigo* (尊敬語)
- Humble: *Kenjōgo* (謙譲語)

Linguistically, the former two honorifics are used for someone who is talked *about*, and the last refers to someone talked *to*.

Each of these types of speech has its own vocabulary and verb endings, posing a real challenge to those that want to achieve true mastery of the language!

Viewed in this light, honorific language shows not only how the Japanese acknowledge hierarchy but also how they strive to express humility. It reflects a culture of social stratification and social rank as well as degrees of expertise or mastery. Being senior or junior—the *senpai-kōhai* relationship found in many contexts be they teams, schools or workplaces—is embedded in most contexts (work, sport, art). The choice of pronoun expresses, among others, the social relationship between the person speaking and the person he or she addresses. Honorific speech is often longer—sometimes much longer—than more "familiar" speech. This can lead to constructions such as the following: *Go-kyōryoku no hodo onegai mōshiagemasu.* I most respectfully request the favour (or pleasure) of your cooperation.

So, merely saying that Japanese is complex does not even begin to describe the challenge of speaking and understanding it beyond just simple conversational settings. A respected Japanese translator of such American authors as John Barth, Masao Shimura, once described Japanese as a "squishy language" in which the absence of assertion is part of the grammatical structure. Instead of saying "I must go now," the Japanese would say, *ikenakereba, naranai*: literally, "if I don't go, it will be bad." Negation is incorporated at the same time that the subject (the first person pronoun) is often omitted creating utterances that seem to "float" without self-referentiality, yet contain self-judgment in the projected act. The disappearance of the grammatical subject seems, at least linguistically, to be another incarnation of obeisance.

As I noted earlier, personal relationships, as well as interactions, reflect relative rank—the distinction between senior (*senpai*) or junior (*kōhai*). The complexity of the Japanese language, therefore, lies primarily in its social nuance. Conveying politeness or deference, for instance, is not as straightforward as using plural versus singular forms (as for instance in the Greek or French language). Take for example Natsume Soseki's classic book titled *I Am A Cat* (*Wagahai Neko De Aru*): The English translation (Soseki, 1972) doesn't come close to the nuance in the phrase as the author uses an archaic form of the pronoun "I" (akin to a royal "We").

The Japanese use of honorifics is perhaps similar to the honorific systems of the Korean language, and in some elements, Chinese—but perhaps more complex than both, expressed through both special vocabulary and unique grammatical forms. As such, it's far from a simple choice of plural versus singular when using pronouns or the French *vous* and *tu* dependent upon intimacy. What makes things even more nuanced (and complicated) is the fact that there is no masculine or feminine forms for nouns. Another peculiarity is that there is a special vocabulary used only in journalism, known as *Shinbun-yōgo*, often taught now in Japanese schools, for repetitive concepts, like "according to."

The importance of harmony, in family and business, is paramount and the language unmistakably reflects this theme. Working in harmony is viewed as essential for productivity, while being indirect and courteous, even in disagreement. This ethos is inculcated in children early on, at home, at school, and then in the workplace.

It is a cultural code of sorts they learn and share. Viewed from this perspective, I wonder if the Japanese "gaps" when engaging in discourse are an attempt to get a dialogue going, by leaving things unfinished while at the same time preserving *wa* or harmony. There are numerous ways to express hesitation or "tentativeness" with empty "fillers" in conversations. Indeed, "spaces" (both literal or metaphorical) may be seen as representing lapsed continuity. They find frequent expression in artifacts (architecture) but also in the language itself. The excessive use of *shikashi* ("but") with nothing following it (no dependent or independent clause in a compound structure) can be construed as an open invitation of sorts. This linguistic dangling may be frustrating to those who see it as an expression of weakness and avoidance (a vice) rather than an attempt at prudence and reserve (a virtue). It creates an asymmetry between what is said and the intention behind it that is somewhat at odds with the Western penchant for directness and clarity and for being definitive in our intentions.

Ambiguity and vagueness increase the degree of "optionality" (affording more choice) while helping maintain harmony. The expression *kūki o yomu* literally means "to read the air" - an ability to understand a situation without an explicit reference. Another expression "*ichi o kiite, jū o shiru*" literally means "know ten from hearing one," again referring to an ability to infer details when only given partial clues.

Indeed, linguistics provides an intriguing perspective through which one can examine cultures, not just as a way of giving expression to social status, but in a way that is reflective of gender and status. In fact, if one views languages through a psychoanalytic (one could call it psycholinguistic) prism, it can provide additional insight into a host of social conventions and practices. Language can be seen as the lens through which we express our feelings, the window through which we can perhaps view the soul.

Take Takeo Doi's *The Anatomy of Dependence* (first published in 1971 and translated into English two years later), which remains one of the best books on the topic. Doi talks about the structure of *amae*, translated into English as "dependence, the desire to be passively loved." He endeavors to explain the concept of emotional and social interdependence, which he believes underpins the Japanese psyche. Bertolt Becht, in another context, once described this passivity in political terms: the "shared" passivity of the co-dependents in a brothel, who, on another level, are competitive rivals for the affections of both customers and owner.

Doi connects *amae* to other key Japanese concepts like *tanin* (others), *enryo* (restraint), *giri* (obligation), and *ninjo* (heart or humanity), while providing examples of *amae* from Japanese history, literature, and everyday life. A fascinating read, but one which could easily stray to "*nihonjin-ron*" (a genre developed by a significant number of Japanese scholars to underscore their perceived "uniqueness"), if carried too far. When Doi describes *amae* as a uniquely Japanese need to be in good favor with, and be able to depend on, the people around oneself, perhaps he's pointing out a national trait. But it's debatable whether this is as unrivalled as he claims. He likens this trait to behaving childishly, assuming that parents will indulge you, and views the ideal relationship as that of the parent-child which affords a degree of closeness sought in most other relationships.

> *The psychological prototype of amae can be found in the psychology of the infant and its relationship to its mother after it has realized that its mother exists independently of itself. As its mind develops, it gradually realizes that itself and its mother have independent existences, and comes to feel the mother as indispensable. It is the craving for close contact thus developed that constitutes amae.* (Doi, 2001: 39)

Doi's theory might suggest that Japanese culture's apparent childishness and penchant for miniaturization (the "chan" applied to females in address or "ko" in naming) may be part of the "craving" or dependency, even in nomination. This is recognized even by adults as in the hordes of *kyoikumamas* dedicated to preparing their children's lunches and obsessing about their schedules and homework.

Another concept that exemplifies how linguistic nuances convey social and cultural norms is the distinction between *honne* and *tatemae*. These two terms describe the contrast between a person's true feelings and desires (*honne* or "true sound") and the behavior and opinions one displays in public (*tatemae*: "built in front" or "façade"), again emphasizing the layers behind the various curtains and screens of the "self."

Honne may be contrary to what's expected by society or what's required according to one's position and circumstances and is often kept hidden, except from one's closest friends. *Tatemae* is what's expected by society and required according to one's position and circumstances, and these feelings may or may not match one's *honne*. In many cases, *tatemae* leads to outright lying in order to avoid exposing true feelings. The *honne-tatemae* distinction is considered to be of paramount importance in Japanese culture.

Some see *honne* and *tatemae* as a cultural necessity resulting from a large number of people living in a comparatively small island nation. Close-knit cooperation and the avoidance of conflict are considered to be of vital importance in everyday life. This may explain why the Japanese tend to go to great lengths to avoid conflict, especially within the context of large groups.

In fact, the conflict between *honne* and *giri* (social obligations) has been one of the most usual narratives in Japanese drama through the ages. The protagonist is seen to be conflicted between carrying out his obligations to his family/feudal lord, or following his heart. The same concept in Chinese culture is called "inside face" and "outside face." They also frequently come into conflict. In the West, clinically since Freud's dynamic of compensation, the repression of the *honne* would be regarded as a potential illness (ultimately leaking out or "de-cathected") but usually elaborated in a pathology of *complexes*. In Japan, the difference is easily incorporated and respected and crucial to everyday social interaction and negotiation. The world is a shadow play of illusions to be negotiated rather than some core sincerity to be elucidated.

As the word "no" is considered impolite, hilarious implications arise when Japanese try to politely tell us that we're woefully wrong about something. Perhaps the most classic example of Japanese understatement and nuanced language: The emperor addressing the nation at the end of WWII phrased the fact that they had been defeated as "not necessarily being on the road to victory"!

Here are selected additional linguistic terms that can hopefully enhance our cultural understanding:

Giri: This refers to a person's sense of obligation to his or her friends, family, and even their employer. It's associated with many social customs in Japan such as women being expected to give chocolate, known as *giri-choco*, to their male bosses, coworkers, and acquaintances on Valentine's Day (the men are supposed to return the favor on so-called White Day a month later, but that doesn't always happen).

Gaman: This is when you put up with an unpleasant situation to avoid disturbing the *wa*. It can take the form of enduring the pain of a broken bone with no more than a normal dose of ibuprofen. Japanese are often asked to bear something or "grit it out," as a matter of character building. Sometimes this involves enduring the seemingly unbearable, demonstrating patience, grit, and dignity.

Enryo: The Japanese concept of *enryo* is a form of reserve that is expressed for the sake of other people. It expresses diffidence, restraint and reserve in contexts such as not talking on the phone while on the bus or train, not taking the last bite of food from the dinner platter, or wearing a gauze mask in public to avoid infecting others with your cold. *Enryo* is a quintessential part of Japanese social etiquette.

Wa: The idea of group harmony is explained clearly in Robert Whiting's *You Gotta Have Wa* (updated in 2009), a great read on an interpretation of Japanese culture through the lens of baseball. In the book's introduction, Whiting says: "The underlying philosophy that differentiates Japan and the United States, in baseball, as well as in their societies as a whole, still exists. The trajectory of *wa* is rarely linear, and sometimes it is impossible to predict whose side of the plate it is going to break on."

In the US, where the game was invented (although the British might take umbrage and claim it comes from "rounders"), it's a national pastime, entertainment, and big business. But in Japan, *beisboru* has a philosophical bent, and the underlying concept of *wa* must be maintained within teams. Naturally, this leads to some hilarious incidents when American players try to make heads or tails of the sport in Japan where tie games are tolerated, tough pregame practices are common, and injured pitchers are encouraged to "play through the pain." Managers from their part ask a potential pinch hitter what kind of condition he is in before inserting him into the lineup (as if he could possibly know or be honest if he did). The practice also suggests the quest for resilience, even among those not in the best position to be honest: a player wanting to play.

Chapter 8

Literature

Literature and culture are closely intertwined. While language provides context to culture and acts as a medium for expressing it, literary works provide an invaluable lens through which we can better understand a society's culture. Japan's distinct literature has the singular ability to immerse the reader in the subjective world of ideas, beliefs, norms, and values and helps reveal its underlying codes and rules.

Yet Hofstede, among other academics, cautions against using literature as a rigorous analytical tool to interpret culture. The individual subjectivity involved, goes his argument, makes it difficult to define broad patterns: "Cultures are not king-size individuals: They are wholes, and their internal logic cannot be understood in terms used for the personality."

While the subjectivity of literary works may render them, in a strict sense, "unrepresentative" of the whole, I'm more inclined to agree with Hanauer (2001) who, in his work on teaching cultural knowledge through reading, considers literature a valuable source of cultural knowledge precisely because it presents a personal interpretation of life and values. He argues:

> *It is widely recognized within the community of applied linguists*
> *that learning a language involves more than just learning to use*
> *a set of linguistic structures. (These) are usually considered and*
> *discussed as cultural factors.*

Japan has a long literary tradition (The *Tale of Genji* predates the first English language novel, *Gulliver's Travels*, written in 1726, by over 700 years), widely regarded as one of the finest in the world. Characterized by ambiguity, innuendo, and the importance of subtext, it often takes a deep dive into our emotions, personal tensions, and dilemmas. Reading between the lines is a skill honed by the Japanese at an early age and Japanese literature richly reflects this in its narratives. What is more, recent writing continues to be heavily preoccupied with the conflicts between tradition and modernity, and as some see it, the loss of cultural identity.

Early Japanese literature saw its genesis in the adoption of the Chinese non-phonetic writing system in the early 8th century. Chinese is a very different language (in virtually all respects), yet the Japanese borrowed and adapted Chinese ideographs (*kanji*), and added two phonetic syllabaries (*hiragana* and *katakana*, each of which has 46 characters) to adapt it to the different pronunciation, grammar, phrase structure, and phonetic rules. *Hiragana* is generally used for Japanese words when they're not written in *kanji*, and for all grammatical devices such as conjugations and particles. It also allows the expression of tense, suffixes following a *kanji* root, and words for which there is no *kanji*.

Katakana is normally used for loan words from foreign languages and onomatopoeia. It may also be used for names of animal and plant species, minerals, company names (like Mitsubishi and Suzuki), and also for giving emphasis. But, for those even modestly familiar with the language, *katakana* conveys both history and culture and in fact, may constitute one of the forms assumed by cultural protectionism. The Western strawberry has a history as *ichigo*, a Japanese word, suggesting a long, native presence in the country. This is to be contrasted with the hated or loved broccoli (ブロッコリ), "coming in" in the *Katakana* used for foreign words. The Japanese customer "reads it" as an import, historically not native to Japan. Hence, language informs and prompts barriers to consumption (if one has not tried it) or the exotic temptation to be an *ichigensan* (a first customer). One could, therefore, argue that the multiple notation systems may constitute a structural barrier to import, but also a possible temptation, simultaneously. I'm told that in some parts of the US, feral pig, wild boar, and javelina all refer to the same beast represented as *inoshishi* in *hiragana*, but with an abundance of representations on winter menus in Japan, including *botan nabe*, which would give the foreigner no possible expectation (even in the hands of a great translator), as the *botan* refers to the shape (of a peony) into which the slices of the wild boar are cut prior to being dipped into the simmering stock of the *nabe*. The *kana* syllabaries convey phonetic sounds or *phonemes* (a consonant followed by a vowel) with each character standing for a syllable. Not knowing what one is about to eat, given that its representation on menus might be obscured by the form in which the subject is presented rather than the subject itself, is a common experience—as opposed to say, eating *coq au vin* in Burgundy where most consumers would recognize the *coq* as an aged fowl.

Each *kanji* character represents a concept or idea and conveys meaning as well as sound. Complicating matters, each character also has one or more "readings" (ways to pronounce it, distinguished between "*on*" and "*kun*"), and the correct one depends on which word the *kanji* is part of. Many also act as stand-alone words. I'm often asked how many *kanji* one must master to be able to read Japanese text. My answer: It depends on what level of proficiency you are aiming at. For popular text, knowledge of around 1,500 *kanji* should suffice, whereas for contemporary literature, you'll need more than 3,000. Now, if your thing is classical literature, even 15,000 *kanji* may not be enough. The Ministry of Education in Japan assumes that high school graduates have mastered the required *kanji* count (1,945), which is used by most newspapers and magazines for their articles.

One of the first expressions of early Japanese literature is the *Manyōshū* ("Collection of Myriad Leaves"), a compilation of Japanese poetry put in written form around the first half of the eighth century. Many Japanese scholars and poets have regarded the *Manyōshū* as the embodiment of the essential characteristics of "Japaneseness," especially the "sense of sadness of things" (*mono no aware*).

Later, in the Heian period, a particular literary form emerged, written by aristocratic women. *Murasaki Shikibu* (Lady Murasaki) wrote *Genji Monogatari* ("Tale of Genji") in the early 11th century. Widely regarded as a masterpiece, it's arguably the world's first novel. In a nostalgic tone, it expresses the sadness of life, and the melancholy associated with good things eventually passing. What never passes, however, is the subtext of whispers, palace intrigue and convoluted patterns of jealousy that threaten to subvert elite taste: an oral component, equally ephemeral, in competition with elaborately refined ideas of aesthetic detachment. Prince Genji, the amorous protagonist, strives to pursue beauty and refinement, the defining virtues of the court, as he deals with their ephemeral nature and those of court intrigue.

Sei Shonagon, another contemporary court lady, wrote *Makura no Soshi* ("The Pillow Book"), an array of notes and reflections that also provides insight into Heian aristocratic life, and its emphasis on elegance and beauty. Unlike *Genji Monogatari*, it is imbued with wit while being more uplifting.

After reading a translated work, foreign readers may wonder what nuances they have missed because they couldn't read it in the original language. This is all the more so for Heian literature which was written for aristocratic ladies for whom there was no need to articulate ideas or situations beyond subtle cues. Having said that, I find it equally intriguing that classics from whatever culture (especially those using ideograms such as China and Japan) can retain their power and quality even if the medium is radically different — although a brilliant translator often helps!

Writing in the New Yorker (May 9, 2013) Roland Kelts, the author of *"Japanamerica: How Japanese Pop Culture Has Invaded the United States"* explains the nuances and complexities involved:

> *The Japanese language derives much of its beauty and strength from indirectness—or what we may regard as vagueness, obscurity, implied meaning or merely nuance. Subjects are often left unmentioned in Japanese sentences, and onomatopoeia, with vernacular sounds suggesting meaning, is something that is difficult if not impossible to convey in English.*

What's more, the vocabulary and grammar used often reflect the person's gender, age, and even his social status, and contain a large variety of confusing personal pronouns. The classical period with its emphasis on tales of life in the imperial court gradually gave way to other motifs during the ensuing feudal period. Indeed, while Kyoto (and prior to that, Nara) had been the center of the Japanese world, power began to shift from the Kansai region to Kanto. The so-called *Edo* period saw power shift to feudal lords (*shoguns*) and was marked by the shogunate's move to Edo (modern-day Tokyo). This was the era of the *samurai* and *geisha* and a rising commercial class.

This period welcomed the flourishing of *haiku*, a very short poetic form. Consisting of just 17 syllables, *haiku* came to embody the Japanese aesthetic with its refined view of nature and emotion. It was perfected by *Matsuo Basho* who published a collection called "The Complete *Haiku*" during the 17th century. *Haiku* is typically rendered in three lines of exactly 5, 7, and 5 syllables each, and always contain a *kigo* (a reference to a specific season) reflecting the Japanese sensitivity to the changing seasons, a deep appreciation of nature, and the awareness of the fleeting nature of life itself. It's said to have started with Buddhist monks, giving expression to Zen spirituality: Always "in the moment," contemplative, and all expressed succinctly in a mere three lines.

As society changed, so did literature. After the ancient and medieval periods, themes began to reflect the issues and tensions of the time, marked by the rising influence of the West. Indeed, after the *Meiji* Reformation, which marked the end of a period of feudal isolation, Japanese literature began to give expression to the tensions between tradition and modernity. During these times of change, interest in literature intensified, particularly in fiction which saw the emergence of some brilliant writers. Two received the Nobel Prize: Yasunari Kawabata in 1968, and Kenzaburo Oe in 1994.

Then there are literary giants such as Junichiro Tanizaki, Yukio Mishima, Kobo Abe, Fumiko Enchi, and Shusaku Endo, to name a few, all making their mark on the Japanese literary scene and beyond. From such a huge number of literary works, it's difficult to choose favorites, but here are some of mine:

Some Prefer Nettles by Junichiro Tanizaki (1929)
In the early 1900s, many Japanese authors tended to be preoccupied with the clash between Western ideas and Japanese traditions. This followed the re-opening of Japan to the West in the 1850s and a period of rapid industrialization and progress. In *Some Prefer Nettles*, Tanizaki addressed this theme through the main character, Kaname, who is "modern" in his attitudes and therefore "Westernized." He goes with prostitutes and encourages his wife to have an affair as if this was an acceptable "Western" solution. He feels trapped in a loveless marriage yet

divorce is not something that he can countenance as it would bring shame and humiliation. Influenced by his father-in-law, he becomes increasingly drawn to Japanese tradition and its values as the narrative digresses onto subjects such as puppet theater and *geisha*.

Parenthetically, I'll note that the later work of Tanizaki, The *Gourmet Club* and the exquisite *Devils in Daylight* is outstanding. The narrative's layers take you beyond Alfred Hitchcock, the reader not quite sure what to believe or expect. What is real and what is not, the distinction between sanity and madness, become hard to disentangle in what is very powerful prose.

Kokoro by Natsume Soseki (1914)

Narrated in the first person, the novel revolves around the themes of loneliness, betrayal, and change. *Kokoro* ("heart" in Japanese) is the story of friendship between a young man and a reclusive elder he meets at the beach and whom he addresses as *Sensei* (literally teacher). Haunted by secrets that have marked his tragic life, *Sensei* begins to confide in his young disciple, confessing indiscretions from his own student days and recounting the intense guilt he felt as a result. In the process, the writer alludes to the chasm between *sensei's* moral anguish and his disciple's inability to really comprehend it.

Written in 1914, shortly after the end of the *Meiji Era* (a period of transition between pre-modern and modern Japan), there is deep symbolism in the way the characters think and behave. Soseki provides insight on how different generations dealt with Japan's modernization and the kinds of dilemmas that emerged as a result. *Sensei* can be seen as representing the Meiji era and the tension between the past and impending modernity, while the young man's transitional period after college can be seen as a metaphor for the *Meiji Era* itself.

Wagahaiwa Neko de Aru (*I Am A Cat*) by Natsume Soseki
The title is masterful, using an arcane pronoun for I (akin to a royal "we" yet more layered), conveying a sense of detachment and superiority by the story's narrator, an unwanted stray cat that now lives in the house of Mr Sneeze, a teacher. This satire deconstructs *Meiji* politics and social norms, particularly those which were borrowed from the West. The feline protagonist observes his master and his friends as they go about their daily lives in the 1920s. The cat observes (and judges) the people as they talk about their work and their relationships and even wander onto subjects such as the differences between East and West. As these interactions unfold, the cat is always present, making its own observations, often contemptuous of the protagonists. In modern Japanese fiction, as in the fables of Aesop and Grimm or the short stories of Kenji Miyazawa, animals often speak and humans often have animal characteristics without any clear delineation of precisely who is speaking. As the first person reference is often omitted in everyday conversation in Japanese, the projection of a human voice onto often inanimate objects (like mountains in Kawabata or mousetraps in Miyazawa) seems a way of humanizing the world even as you deny a "self."

The narrator's view of Mr Sneeze can be described as both critical and contemptuous. He is an English teacher in his forties with a wife and three daughters. He comes across as rather silly and inept, partly as a consequence of being isolated. Like Kawabata's protagonist of *Snow Country*, he ostensibly "teaches" the language of a country he has never been to. He spends his free time alone in his study pretending to work hard, yet achieves very little: the most obvious comparison is Mr. Bennet of Jane Austen's *Pride and Prejudice*, equally burdened by three daughters, perhaps indicating Soseki's time as a student of Western Literature. Any disturbance irritates him as it compels him to disrupt his state of perpetual idleness. On one such occasion, he gets annoyed when he is asked to help his wife write a list of things stolen in a burglary to be handed to the police. The novel clearly satirizes Japanese so-called intellectuals of the time, and mirrors their condescending attitude toward others (especially those not in their class) and even toward others in their own family.

In contrast to Soseki and his literary style was Yukio Mishima's darker style. A highly regarded yet controversial author, Mishima is said to have been a contender for the Nobel Prize in Literature. His writing is filled with black humor, strained relationships and dark themes. *Death in Midsummer and Other Stories* is a powerful collection of his short prose, selected by himself. The lead story, "Death in Midsummer" is about human grief and psychological torment, reminiscent of Tolstoy's masterpiece *The Death of Ivan Ilych*. Full of psychological complexity and nuance, his prose is elegant, sometimes even humorous, yet quite dark. I can only wonder how difficult it must have been for the translators to convey the intended meaning and nuance in a linguistic medium so different from the original.

Mishima was a tragic character himself—as conflicted and complex as any found in his books. He was an actor, writer, model, playwright, and poet. He was gay but also drawn to right-wing political (many would say fascist) views. Among his stories is the tale of a monk, poised on the brink of enlightenment and transcendence, at which point he is drawn back into the mortal world by the sight of a royal concubine. Mishima also provides a highly detailed account of a Japanese lieutenant's ritual suicide (*seppuku*)—that was virtually re-enacted by Mishima in his own death by *seppuku* when he was 45.

Recent Modern Literature

Haruki Murakami has become vastly popular the world over through his bestsellers *Kafka On the Shore*, *Dance Dance Dance*, and *Norwegian Wood*, stories of protagonists trying to find themselves and interacting with a variety of interesting characters and their soul-searching.

Kafka On The Shore (2002) by Haruki Murakami

Kafka on the Shore is a novel embodying many of the characteristics of Haruki Murakami's literary creations. A master of alternative realities, often delving into the supernatural, Murakami has captured the imagination of a vast international readership. In fact, he was considered a strong contender for the 2014 Nobel Prize in Literature. The novel contains themes, which appear to fascinate the author: animals that appear to know more than humans; references to classical music and pop culture; protagonists who have lost their way and are on a quest to discover meaning; and the metaphysical questions surrounding our existence.

The Wind-Up Bird Chronicle (1995) by Haruki Murakami

This is perhaps the most famous of Murakami's works. After protagonist Toru Okada's cat runs away he finds himself embroiled in a plot that completely unsettles his boring life and reveals a host of emotional issues. This book earned the author multiple awards and widespread recognition as one of the world's best novelists.

The plot has been described as "labyrinthine" by some for good reason. It involves a bizarre group of characters—a missing cat, a missing wife, a psychic prostitute, an old war veteran—and all kinds of allies and antagonists. At the heart of Murakami's achievement, is an exploration of the various forms of boredom endemic to Japanese culture, especially in his lovely short stories, e.g., a mid-twenties company executive who does the same thing every day, moves from one indifferent girlfriend to another, all of whom dress and act alike, and then finally commits suicide by slashing his wrists in a bathtub. Repetitive life, peculiar to lifetime employment and adherence to a hierarchical system of obedience, is not radically dissimilar from death. Boredom is a form of "loading time" and having too much of it on one's hands.

Kitchen by Banana Yoshimoto (1988)

Kitchen is a fascinating story about an unconventional Japanese family and the way they deal with love and loss. The "mother" is a transgender bar hostess (at a gay nightclub), the son (Yuichi) is a college student who suffers from frequent bouts of melancholy. They take into their home Mikage, Yuichi's classmate, who's just lost her grandmother, the only family she had left. "Kitchen" represents Mikage's comfort zone, the place she uses to become closer to her new "family" and show them appreciation. She learns how to cook, and makes it her passion, helping her cope with her loss and pain: "Perhaps because to me a kitchen represents some distant longing engraved on my soul." The kitchen surely represents a relationship between institutions of imprisonment (a woman's dependency) and simultaneously the possibility of creatively finding a space in which to be inventive. The "kitchen" becomes a new bedroom in which to please oneself and others, simultaneously: the "adopted" (Mikage) inventively "adapts."

The novel is full of unconventional characters, whose emotions Yoshimoto conveys in a most artful way. Society finds it difficult to understand and accept their lifestyle, but the protagonists do their best to be there for each other and deal with grief and adversity.

In this short sampling of Japanese literature, I tried to convey the richness of expression and the powerful underlying themes that drive their narrative. I'm often intrigued by the ability of translators (such as Jay Rubin, Edwin McClellan, and John Nathan) to convey the intended nuances in Western languages. Reading in the original *kanji* allows ample alliteration, onomatopoeia and different grades of honorific versus familiar language, chosen carefully to reflect the social situation, all of which need to be conveyed in different, one could say less powerful, ways in another language. Yet, millions across the world derive joy from such translated works. James Hobbs, who teaches at Iwate Medical University, describes the challenge in an insightful way:

> *When looking at a translation of a text rooted in a foreign culture, it may often be possible to find gaps, or to suggest changes that will produce a closer semantic resemblance to the original, but it will never be possible to produce a translation that accounts for each and every one of the features that made the original text worthy of being read. To say that the translator's work is finished suggests only that no more can be done to improve the translation. In essence, the translator strives to bridge the cultural gap between readers and the foreign text that lies beyond their reach.*

When Murakami's long-time translator Jay Rubin was asked about the peculiar challenges of translating the great master's work, he noted (Sehgal, 2011):

> *One is freer in translating from Japanese than from Western languages because there are no cognates or other familiar guideposts to which one feels constrained to adhere. It's more like creating the text from scratch rather than transferring phrases and sentences from one language into another, probably more fun.*

In fact, Jay Rubin must feel somewhat weighed down by the fact that the master whose work he translates is an accomplished translator himself. In the course of his long career, Murakami not only wrote but translated no fewer than 70 published works, mostly modern American novels. He particularly liked Raymond Carver, John Irving, and Salinger and credited these translations with developing him as a writer. In fact, he wrote the opening pages of his own book *Hear the Wind Sing*, in English and then translated those pages into Japanese, just to see "how that would sound."

Chapter 9

Education

Many of the cultural lenses discussed here are most relevant to Japan's educational system and its underlying philosophy of the what, how and why we learn and by whom. It's driven by the firm belief that education trumps class and privilege as the key factor behind success (even if, as I explain later, class and wealth do help shape educational attainment to varying degrees). Indeed, getting into Tokyo or Kyoto Universities, or any of the other top-tier universities, is purely a matter of scoring well on exams. No consideration is given to connections, social standing, or where the parents went to school. No essays to write where you can weave in your background experiences and life story. Just a "hellish" exam result! Although this has the appearance of a meritocracy, some would argue that it is often not entirely so. The children of the well-educated have sufficient monetary support to go to the best *yobiko* (cram schools) and hence have a "leg up" on the dreaded entrance exams, much as in the pre-war and immediate post-war years, the most affluent students in the US or the UK attended elite private boarding schools. The *yobiko* cram schools are in fact, like the Choate School or Eton, a streaming system directing the future student to the kind of exam (and the exam format) on which he or she is most likely to succeed.

One of the political debates following the death of George H.W. Bush, the 41st President of the United States, has centered around the perceived demise of a genuine American meritocracy that benefited from elite prep schools and the *de rigueur* Ivy League education. With the encroachment of Catholics, Jews (previously restricted to quotas for admission), and minority students following upon the heels of affirmative action upon elite institutions, the social elitism of "narrow tent" Protestantism (the original WASPS) has been eroded. Ambition to get ahead has replaced, so the argument goes, a certain *noblesse oblige*, which included government service as an obligation, as part of one's education. There was post-1945 a perceived need to assimilate "bright, but socially disadvantaged" students into the elite classes, much as England did with various schemes like the Colombo Scholarships extended to the far reaches of a dwindling Empire, to the geographically disadvantaged.

As a relatively homogenous, aspirational middle-class country in terms of income and social prestige after World War II (and land reform initiated under Occupation) Japan had less need to open its educational doors to wider access by underprivileged social minorities. Hence education at elite universities has less to do with acquiring an education (learned after one has been hired upon graduation at the hands of a company *senpai/kōhai* apprenticeship program), and more to do with socialization, the "activities" of extra-curricular club life. Just as "life" at elite universities often centered around the Skull & Bones Club at Yale, the Tiger Club at Princeton, the Hasty Pudding Club at Harvard, or the activities described in the novels of Evelyn Waugh at Oxford, so in Japan there is an "old boys network" attached to the best national universities, with Tokyo and Kyoto Universities at the forefront. Participation in these activities may be a more important indicator of future success than one's grades at the institution. The decline of meritocracy in Europe has been written about in *The Rise and Fall of European Meritocracy* by Ivan Krastev in *The International New York Times* (Jan. 18, 2017, p. 14).

Perhaps the first thing to note about education in Japan is how early it commences, under a variety of formats and how long it (potentially) continues. Groups of infants still in diapers are often encountered in the wheeled cages on sidewalks being towed about for fresh air and the observation of life around them. Young parents consistently complain about the shortage of day-care facilities and the restrictions this shortage poses for mothers eager to re-enter the workforce after giving birth. And many women in their eighties are students of *ikebana* or *shodō* (calligraphy), or design through an abundance of *senmongaku* (specialized schools and tutors outside the formal education system) which grant diplomas.

In an attempt to remedy the sharply lower birth rate—now nowhere near replacement level—the *Diet* has tentatively approved in May of 2019 a bill providing enhanced support in the form of subsidies. These "allowances" will range from 22,000 yen (about $250) for a public pre-kindergarten to 31,000 yen (about $340) monthly for privately-run ones. These allotments are dependent upon an increase in the 8% consumption tax to 10%, previously postponed twice due to the deleterious impact upon consumer spending. Previously earmarked to reduce debt as an austerity measure, the LDP and its coalition partners have perhaps begun to realize that adding young women to the workforce while assisting enhanced pre-school education is an acceptable "trade-off."

The *gimukyoiku* (compulsory education) period is nine years: six in *shōgakko* (elementary school), and three in *chūgakko* (junior high school). Even though high school (*kōkō*) is not compulsory, most pupils continue. Indeed, high school enrollment is over 96% nationwide and nearly 100% in cities. The educational system guarantees a very high standard, producing one of the world's best-educated youth, with 100% enrollment in compulsory grades and no illiteracy.

Indeed, the evidence from international rankings such as OECD's Program for International Student Assessment (PISA) suggests that the Japanese are doing something right. One successful practice is incorporating *senmongakkos* into the educational system. These institutions are essentially trade schools, operating outside both the formal education system and the various *yobikos* or cram schools. For those unable to afford or otherwise adapt to the rather rigid and increasingly expensive formal education sector, these schools specialize in instruction in a variety of skills that can presumably be monetized, ranging from household and industrial plumbing to kimono design. So, these practices have lead to some impressive stats:

- Japan ranked second among OECD advanced nations in "science literacy" in 2015, up from fourth in 2012
- Fifth in "mathematical literacy," up from seventh
- Eighth in reading comprehension (remember, we are dealing with *kanji* here), down from fourth.

On the other hand, global English proficiency rankings may be somewhat misleading. On comprehension, composition, and communication (taken as a composite), Japanese high school students scored the second lowest of any country in the world, earning the condemnation of the 2nd to last place finish. You ask "Who was last?" The Democratic People's Republic of Korea (North Korea), which did have isolation as a possible excuse. Despite the poor results on a test administered internationally, Japan spends more money on English language learning than any other country in the world, if the tuition of cram schools, *jukus*, and assorted private institutions dedicated to exam preparation, is taken into account. A vibrant commercial industry is the production of English textbooks and sample exam questions for instructors at *yobikos* and other cram schools. These "cram books" are often authored by retired university professors of English who reap royalties from their production. As they previously devised and graded entrance exams for their universities, students, teachers, book producers, and the cram schools are part of a self-reflexive system: there were eight of them within a ten-minute walk of our residence.

While Japanese students may score well when asked to translate English passages into their own language, they're practically hopeless when it comes to actual speaking. Apart from those who are lucky to be taught by *gaijin* English teachers (especially those who are native speakers), most students learn from teachers who know *about* the language, yet struggle to put a complete sentence together. English as taught is in effect a "dead language," used only for the singular purpose of university admissions. The closest comparison might be required Latin classes in the mid-1950s in the United States for "university track" students. And the pedagogical rationale is somewhat similar: it helps you to learn other (*Romance*) languages or become "more international." It resembles the late Victorian and Edwardian period in the United Kingdom when it was thought that elite women from good families should learn to play the piano as a "gateway" skill to both other instruments and (more importantly) attracting the attention of a future husband to their cultivated skills.

After years in Japan, it dawned on me that English teachers (most of whom have a poor command of conversational English) prefer to talk *about* English, rather than actually teach students to *speak* English. They'd rather talk about the supposed importance of the distinction between "ought to" and "must" (who gives a fig— pardon the French—for this useless debate), which is the antithesis of how modern linguists believe you should learn a language.

An American friend told me of his first experience in Tokyo as an English teacher. When asked to give a teaching demo at a popular (and exorbitantly priced) language school, he practiced a brief dialogue with another teacher in front of a group of 20 rapt students. Then, the main teacher took over and spoke for no less than 20 minutes, explaining the grammatical vagaries of the four-line dialogue—all in Japanese. It would be difficult to devise a more effective way to turn pupils off from learning a language! Perhaps this is one reason Japanese graduates tend to place last in the world on the "TOEFL-IBT speaking."

Yet, one of the questions regarding educational attainment figures is how illiteracy can be non-existent with such a complex writing system. As I explained earlier, in addition to *kanji*, the Japanese have *hiragana* and *katakana*, two sets of phonetic script or syllabaries each with 46 characters. These represent syllables (usually including a consonant and a vowel like "*ka*"). These characters express all the sounds of modern Japanese: *hiragana* used together with *kanji* to write ordinary Japanese words; *katakana* used to write words introduced from other languages, names of foreign people and places, sounds, and animal cries.

Of course, not all is rosy as a mere result of literacy. There's a downside to the incessant pursuit of achievement and excellence. Yes, the Japanese system produces highly literate and numerate young people who go on to work hard to earn a living, but there are definite shortcomings. Indeed, *The Japan Times* carried an article titled "The educational system has much to learn" on September 30, 2017:

> *There is a driven, compulsive quality to Japanese education, which emerges clearly in a report by Shukan Toyo Keizai magazine titled "Schools are breaking down." Technological progress has a side-effect: An economy that demands higher and higher education is the price of admission into it. Children struggle to learn, and teachers to teach, more and more. Two resulting symptoms are overworked teachers and bullied, or bullying, children.*

One can see a pattern here throughout one's life: pressure at education spills into pressure at work, later on, resulting in people literally working themselves to death.

In his seminal book on education in Japan, *Learning to Bow*, Bruce Feller describes the year he spent in a small rural Japanese town as an English teacher. He discovered how codependent Japanese culture is, and how every decision must be made in a group context. An example he cites is of a girl who grew up in Japan and then lived in Peru for some years. When she came back, the Japanese students didn't know how to respond to or deal with her and simply cut her out of their lives. The girl suffered from a strong sense of culture shock and felt as though she didn't belong anymore. This suggests, of course, a continuous difficulty in the assimilation of those (natively) "us" in a culture whose commercial products have penetrated international markets with great success. One might ask rhetorically if this difficulty represents a distrust of those who are even slightly "internationalized"? What is less determinable is whether the girl was an object of envy by her fellow students (given her life experience) or the victim of the neglect of which some Americans in rural areas of the country feel toward the "elites" on both coasts. Isolation of the "other" (even if "me" ethnically) can be either envy or prejudice toward one who has been tainted, or both simultaneously, in a culture that values an elusive purity, even in aesthetic design.

Feiler contends that Japanese education is much more rigorous than others. Students go to school an average of 100 days per year more than in the US. There's a high level of stress placed on students in Japan to compete to get a great education and succeed. As noted earlier, the term *kyoiku mama* describes many overzealous Japanese mothers obsessed with educational achievement and upward mobility.

My own wife's preoccupation with educational attainment caused occasional arguments over what I sometimes saw as excessive pressure on our daughter until she was awarded silver and bronze medals at successive Math Olympiads and got into Cambridge (BSc) and Oxford (MSc) to study neuroscience. She's a lovely, gracious, and generous person, yet seems to lack a degree of "street sense" or guile. A degree of gullibility may be one of the trade-offs one makes when prioritizing academic achievement, as we did. So is the freedom to take up pursuits that help us relax and socialize. I'm sure many of the children who are subjected to "tough love" yearn for the opportunity to be "just another kid," free from the huge expectations that are placed on them, and in some ways readier to face the challenges of a world that isn't all rosy and fair.

My wife has some "tiger mom" in her (see *Tiger Moms* by Princeton's Amy Chua, on the rigorous education pushed by a Chinese-American mom on her two daughters), a true *kyoiku mama*. In that sense she is quite typical in her homeland, where the pressure they place on their children perhaps explains the high standard of education and some typical success traits: discipline and grit (one example is wearing shorts as part of their uniforms, even in the dead of winter) by providing a constant "wind beneath their wings" that can be enormously helpful and stifling at the same time. Indeed the national fixation on attainment (culminating in "examination hell") could lead to well-documented pathologies and social clumsiness. Feelings of alienation from not meeting high expectations drive the high suicide rates (by international standards), while juvenile delinquency continues to be a serious problem.

I should note here that Japan's fixation with educational attainment while nearing extreme levels, may actually be somewhat typical in East Asia. If that were ever possible you may wonder! Indeed, Koreans have taken exam anxiety to a different level with the entire country grinding to a halt on the day of the nationwide university entrance exams (Moon, 2018):

Today, almost 600,000 South Korean students sit the College Scholastic Ability Test, a gruelling set of university entrance exams that typically takes the whole day. It is difficult to overstate the significance of the CSAT. Similar to other global standardized exams, CSAT scores open doors to prestigious universities. In Korea, however, social pressure to get into the three top universities (known as the "SKY" colleges) is beyond intense. Only 1% of students make it through, a virtual ticket to success in their future career. For that single day, the whole nation comes to a stand-still. Work starts an hour later to allow students to get to their testing centers on time; planes are grounded during the listening portion of the exam so as not to create any distractions. Parents and grandparent, pray for their children's success, joined by their extended family.

Unlike the West, where failure at an entrance exam may end your future chances of entering a particular university, in Japan this is not the case. Young people are allowed to retake a given university's entrance exam year after year, paying rather high fees for the privilege. At certain second- and third-tier private universities, these fees make up a substantial part of revenue. These so-called *rōnin* (the term used for "masterless samurai," in the sense that they are not in the formal school system) enroll in exam preparation schools (known as *yobiko*) until they manage to get in (or eventually give up after they realize they can't, possibly after 3 or more tries). It is not unusual to be a *ronin* for several years! My own nephew recently got into Tokyo University (an elusive dream for the vast majority of young Japanese) after spending a year as a *ronin* and hedging his bets by applying to Keio and Waseda universities (top tier private Universities). I sent him a warm congratulatory note to which he replied immediately with a most gracious and humble tone but then added something typically Japanese, signifying absolute grit and determination that he will not let us all down: "I'll work hard for my future." The intent was unmistakable and could be paraphrased as: "rest assured that I'll grab this opportunity by the horns and make a success of it."

◇◇◇

My brother-in-law Dr. Akira Suzuki and son Tomoki at Tokyo University's
"entrance ceremony" for freshmen.
(Photo by author)

Those who conceive of higher education as simply another consumer product (albeit with niche status for those gaining entrance to the Rolex equivalent), the system seems incredibly inefficient and increasingly expensive when various cram schools are factored into the cost. There is incredible pressure to gain entrance to the best "brands," which are invariably oversubscribed whereas the lower echelons of tertiary education in Japan have a surplus of spaces. The over-expansion of education in Japan following World War II, combined with a declining birth rate, has pressured mergers and "consortiums" among institutions of higher education that were previously independent, all in the interests of enhancing economies of scale. There are probably too many universities in the country. Rather well-known private universities in Japan—such as Ritsumeikan in Kyoto—now advertise both locally and internationally in an attempt to remain competitive.

While largely egalitarian and high quality, it would be an oversimplification to characterize Japanese education as free from the tensions of privilege and disparity, especially in the last two decades. Oxford University Sociology Professor Takehiko Kariya refers to the "inflation of education credentials" and its resultant inequity as a serious problem, which was partly an unintended consequence of the privatization policies pursued by the government.

Kariya contends that the globalization of higher education has proceeded hand-in-hand with the globalization of the workforce, as people travel abroad to receive their education and to seek employment. This leads to a corresponding decrease in the advantage bestowed on a degree holder in the job market, similar in some ways to price inflation, as it marks the decline in the value of certain degrees.

Chapter 10

The Legal System

After the *Meiji* Restoration, the Japanese set out to modernize their country by learning (and then adopting/adapting) a variety of practices from the West. They did this after carefully evaluating prevailing models in the most advanced parts of the world (continental Europe and the US) and selecting those they felt were fit for purpose, considering the Japanese context. The legal system that best fit their criteria was that of continental Europe, especially Germany. Indeed, the drafters of the Japanese Civil Code of 1896 based them largely on the German Civil Code. Subsequent revisions were meant to complete the transition to the continental European model.

As a result of the post-World War II occupation, Japanese law evolved in some respects to mirror certain principles taken from the United States. For example, the examination of witnesses in civil cases followed US legal thinking as did aspects of labor and corporate law. So, Japan's current legal system is a hybrid of Western European (especially German) and American law, which historically drew on English common law.

Two relatively recent adaptations of western legal conventions might be illustrative. In May of 2009, Japan adopted a "lay judge" system in which ordinary citizens work alongside professional judges in criminal trials, so as to presumably "promote public understanding of the judiciary through citizen participation." Six lay judges sit alongside three professional judges and hand down a ruling by majority decision. Although 70% of the people summoned either did not respond to the summons or were excused due to other obligations (work), 90,000 people have participated. The introduction of the lay judge system has nonetheless brought about change that most citizens view positively: 1) the use of video recordings of interrogations; 2) the introduction of pre-trial "discovery" procedures in which the issues at hand are narrowed, producing speedier trials with fewer delays; 3) the participation of lay judges not only in judgments but in the sentencing phase of those found guilty, one effect of which would be an evaluation of "community impact" of the crime. One result has been an increase in "suspended sentences" (probation) which would condition ultimate judgment upon successful rehabilitation (a genuinely sincere *gomen nasai*).

The second adaptation, used in the recent indictment of Carlos Ghosn, the former CEO of Nissan, is the use of "plea bargaining," previously unknown in Japanese jurisprudence. Associates of the suspect who may be under indictment *for* or abetted *in* the crime are offered the opportunity to plead guilty to a lesser charge in return for cooperating with the prosecution. Enacted in June of 2018, this provision gives prosecutors an additional tool in ferreting out conspiracies as well as reducing the number of trials, while recycling the testimony of those willing to cooperate in return for a lighter or suspended sentence.

There are five types of courts: the Supreme Court, High Courts, District Courts, Family Courts, and Summary Courts. The elements, which were taken from the German imperial model, explain why the courts are actually involved in investigating facts. The US system, on the other hand, explains some of the more adversarial elements. One of the criticisms of the resultant system is the great latitude given to prosecutors.

For the most part, Japan remains a civil law country as opposed to, say US, England, and India, which are regarded as common law countries. The main difference is that in common law countries, case law (published judicial opinions) are of critical importance since most law is uncodified (no comprehensive legal rules and statutes), whereas in civil law systems (Germany, France, China) codified statutes govern legal interpretation. Over time, legal systems came to borrow elements from the less dominant system on which they were originally based.

Elliott Hahn's *Overview of the Japanese Legal System* (Hahn, 1983) is a great reference on the topic. It notes that given that the traditional Japanese legal system (prior to Meiji) was based on Confucian principles, the Western emphasis on the rights and duties of the parties delineated by a contract is still viewed perhaps as less important than preserving harmony between the parties (*wa*). Hahn also notes that it is misleading to compare the raw number of attorneys practicing in Japan with the number in the United States. We often hear that there are (in the West) twenty five times as many attorneys per capita as in Japan but whilst this is strictly true it reflects differences in context as well as definitions.

The Japanese permit many people who are not attorneys, but quasi-lawyers, to perform tasks we normally associate with attorneys. One type of quasi-lawyer in Japan is the "judicial scrivener," who may draft court documents, transfer title to land and give legal advice in these matters. Then there is the "administrative scrivener," who may draft legal documents for submission to government offices. There are also the *benrishi* and *zeirishi*. *Benrishi* have the power to give legal advice on patent and trademark matters and even may represent clients in court. *Zeirishi* have the power to give legal advice in tax matters and to represent their clients before the Tax Office. Attorneys and public accountants qualify as *zeirishi*. Others must pass an exam to be accredited either as *zeirishi* or as *benrishi*. Finally, there is the quasi-lawyer class comprised of university graduates who specialized in law during their university studies and now work in corporate or governmental legal departments. In the Japanese university system, unlike that of most American universities and colleges, students can specialize in law, taught by law professors.

I have already touched upon corporate governance in Japan and I would be remiss if I did not include a reference to its legal implications in the context of Japan's legal system. Indeed, from an institutional and legal perspective, corporate governance reforms began in the 1990s which included changes in the relevant laws (a new company law, for instance, incorporated the revised commercial code) and institutional settings. Whittaker and Deakin (2009) contend that while these attempts at reform are still evolving, they have not really re-shaped managerial mentality. Such a shift would have required not just legal and institutional corporate governance reforms but also associated changes in management practices which have remained rather difficult to change to an appreciable extent. The authors concluded that the Japanese experience suggests that there are limits to the global convergence of company law principles and practices and that the association of the Anglo-American model with the "modernization" of corporate governance may have been misplaced.

Law and Order

Historically, crime in Japan has been comparatively low, and the crime rate has even been dropping over the past few decades. A Japan Times article (January 2018) titled *Japan's crime rate hits a record low as the number of thefts plummets* quotes police data on the drastic fall in recorded crimes:

The number of recorded crimes in Japan continued to fall in 2017, hitting a record low of 915,111 on the back of a sharp drop in thefts… The overall number of cases has consistently declined in Japan after hitting a peak of 2.85 million in 2002…In 2016 the figure dropped below the 1 million mark for the first time since the end of World War II, to 996,120.

In the face of falling crime rates, police now have more time to deal with matters that they would have perhaps ignored in the past. Gropers (*chikan*) tended to be ignored unless their offense was particularly egregious, but recently lay judges have tended to be more strict on sexual crimes and offenses. Now, incidents are more likely to be pursued not only because the police may have less to do, but also because the "me too" movement in the West has raised public awareness. Indeed, the Japanese appear to have become somewhat less tolerant of harassment and deviant behavior, dismissed in the past as objectionable (and perhaps sick) but rather benign.

In trying to explain differences in terms of crime and violence, a study in the *British Journal of Criminology* (1999) titled "A cultural study of the low crime rate in Japan" looked at several possible causes. One of these was that group formation in Japan is based on geographic location (i.e. it is "locality based"). This creates a sense of security but at the expense of having to adhere to an extensive set of rules (which many regard as rather repressive). These two elements produce a high level of self-control, which in turn tends to restrain people from committing crimes. The author contrasts this with the West's emphasis on group formation based on personal attributes coupled with two other important factors: the limited and permissive nature of their rules and the relative freedom of action.

Historically, British law has perhaps been acutely aware of the role of public opinion as a kind of appellate division of the law, from the time of A.V. Dicey's seminal *Law and Public Opinion in*

Nineteenth-Century England (1910). Given a hierarchical society, social reputation would be sullied when the patriarchy and its often ne'er-do-well scions ran afoul of the law, imagined as loss of the self-control that defines a privileged class. Hence "going to law," like the resort to "money-lenders" (as opposed to discreet family bankers having its correlate in the dubious "salaryman loan" schemes in Japan) by the suddenly financially indebted, becomes a literal "dis-grace." It "exposes" both defendants and plaintiffs to public knowledge—and hence enhanced circulation—of *judicially negotiated* settlement as opposed to social harmony. Dicey refers to "public opinion" as a "cross-current" which both infects the legislative making of the law and, ironically, gives a more public, extrajudicial verdict as too harsh or too lenient.

If the ink-smudged scriveners and endless delays of Dickens' Chancery in *Bleak House* were not warning enough, Trollope's *Parliamentary Novels* are a cautionary note about the need for the avoidance of the law that still prevails in both Great Britain and Japan. When the Duke of Silverbridge (in *The Duke's Children*) wishes to choose an American wife not approved by his father, the Duke of Omnium and a Liberal Party Prime Minister. His father grants permission for the international marriage only after warning his son to "never go to law, for it is ruination even if you prevail given your class." One might compare this strategic avoidance of the law with an American President who, before surely adding to the total after his election in 2016, had been a plaintiff or defendant in over 4,000 legal actions! Social harmony or enhanced divisiveness may be affected by how we regard the law: as remedy or illness.

The *koban* system, a distinct form of neighborhood policing, involves routine visits to households. A rule of thumb is for a police officer to "oversee" roughly 500 households in his "beat." This might suggest a more "custodial" relationship between the police and neighborhood residents, including more frequent contact to warn of disasters or scams targeting older citizens who may not have all their wits about them. To be sure, the "koban system" of attentive neighborhood police boxes (usually manned by two officers) can be abused, as apparently was the case during World War II when they often spied upon suspected collaborators. "Caring" and "spying"—forms of informational exchange after all—may be the unacknowledged predecessor of today's various "platforms" which monetize information about consumer preferences!

Because the judicial system is not entirely distinguishable from the government (unlike the supposed separation of legislative, judicial, and executive branches in the West) in criminal or civil cases in Japan, a recent area of attention has been directed toward what in the West is termed "class action lawsuits." The plaintiffs in these cases—often involving environmental pollution (noise, industrial contamination of waterways, atmospheric particulate matter)—would be the public at large, and hence a collective. *Kyōsantō* (the Communist Party of Japan) have taken an intense interest. Approved as a legitimate party and allowed to campaign freely under McArthur's occupation following World War II (uniquely in the Asian context) with modest success in local elections and coalition partners, it functions much like "Green Parties" do in Europe. In the absence of a profit motive that might attract civil or criminal lawyers, *Kyōsantō* seeks a "representative interest" that might be leveraged for political advantage rather than legal determination.

* * *

The different norms that govern the circumstances under which violence may be justified also explains the very low rate in police violence, again in sharp contrast to the US or even Western Europe. This may be seen as a reflection of the Confucian values of conformity and group harmony, which lead to an enlightened view of authority.

Another dimension of criminality that is quite distinctive is the different philosophy that governs corrections and imprisonment. US prison populations are much larger and tend to be much more violent. Prosecutors in Japan have considerable discretion on how they handle individual cases and are generally very reluctant to bring charges, and when these are brought, they prefer suspended sentences to incarceration. And even in cases when a felon is put behind bars, the system is less punitive and more geared toward rehabilitation (through education, training, and counselling) rather than punishment.

Understandably, the Carlos Ghosn saga brought considerable international scrutiny to Japan's criminal justice system. Most criticism was on procedural (not comparative fairness) grounds and whether he was accorded "due process." An article in the UK's *Independent* (December 23, 2018) titled *Carlos Ghosn may be guilty—but the Japanese criminal justice system is in the dock too* took issue with prosecutorial power. It noted:

> *It appeared that Ghosn was going to be released on bail last week, but fresh evidence produced by prosecutors at the last minute has kept him detained this weekend. In Japan, suspects can be re-arrested on different allegations, which restarts the clock again on their maximum 23-day detention. Ghosn has not even been formally charged yet.*

The article then goes on to quote Colin Jones, a professor of Doshisha Law School in Kyoto that "detention is essentially an investigative tool used to interrogate suspects and develop evidence." But this would not be much different from a common practice of car ferry British travelers to Spain in the 1960s–70s who had to buy extra insurance to cover "bailed release" if involved in a traffic accident: Spanish authorities jailed drivers until blame could be assessed after any vehicle accident. The idea was that evidence could be contaminated if the parties were free!

The Ghosn case took a rather unexpected turn of late, when he managed to escape from house arrest in Tokyo, ending up in Lebanon. Rather than fleeing justice, he tried to portray his audacious escape as fleeing from a "rigged" justice system that somehow conspired against him: a victim rather than the criminal that the court judged him to be.

In fact, given that the evidence of financial malfeasance was overwhelming, this embarrassing affair only proves that the initial decision to deny him bail was correct. His past deeds and character did suggest that he was a definite flight risk (the bail decision was later reversed once he engaged a new legal team) and that genuine contrition was rather alien to his disposition.

In a "shame culture" such as Japan's, Ghosn's cowardly flight brings embarrassment to those of us who have made the country our second physical or spiritual home: a contagion of shame which will take time to shake off. Perhaps it should not be this way, but it assuredly is, because stereotypes are often the only proxy for the character of the "Other."

Chapter 11

Clouds Over Future Sunrises

Lifelong employment was one of the foundations of Japanese industrial and labor relations for many years. While it had its drawbacks, it created a dedicated, engaged workforce essential to Japanese competitiveness in the boom years. Employee retention was high with all the benefits that came with it. Of course, lifelong employment had its downside as well, especially when operating flexibility was constrained by rigid arrangements in economically lean times, requiring quick adaptation and downsizing.

Then came the lost decade, beginning a trend, which at least partly diluted the employer-employee social contract. Contingent or alternative employment became more common, affording flexibility to both employers and employees, but creating a climate of job insecurity and weakened loyalty. This is the so-called "gig economy." At the same time, new forms of inequality have emerged in what Oxford University Professor Takehiro Kariya terms the "gap society" (*kakusa shakai*). He contends that these new forms of inequality are complex and are caused by a variety of factors resulting in inequality in labor and employment, in welfare and family, in education and social mobility, in the urban-rural divide, as well as in gender. In short, there is now a high degree of inequality in terms of opportunities and outcomes, and this is likely to get more pronounced. Indeed, the global economic competition and governmental policies to cut labor costs and increase labor mobility have led to an increasingly polarized workforce between groups of high- and low-skilled workers and the gradual decline of the "salaryman" stereotype, one who receives a steady monthly salary for life.

The Demographic Time Bomb

While Japan's geography and settlement patterns (mountainous, high-density conurbations) place natural limits on rapid population growth, a decline in population is, in fact, the current challenge.

Today, Japan has fewer than three people of working age for each retiree. By 2030, it will have fewer than two. The challenges are obvious: Fewer than two workers will have to produce and finance consumption for themselves, their personal dependents, and half a retiree.

> *Today we have 2.57 workers supporting each senior citizen. But in 2060, the ratio will be just 1.19 workers per senior. This will put a huge burden on the younger generation. Compare the ageing ratios of different countries: Italy, Sweden, Spain, Germany, France, the UK, the United States, and many developing nations are heading toward populations with 25 or 30 per cent being over 65. But Japan is far ahead of the world.* (Edahiro, 2015)

If the population continues to age at the current rate, the country's economy could face a severe fiscal crisis. The traditionally high savings rate must fall, and the Japanese public will no longer be able to absorb the large amount of debt the government is amassing.

Japan must find ways to supplement its shrinking pool of productive, tax-paying, pension-contributing workers to avoid future problems. But this is problematic in light of the country's cultural aversion to allowing more foreigners in, coupled with the rising retirement age. It also calls for encouraging more women to work. On both of these issues, I foresee a gradual change in attitude. I just hope it will not be too late by the time the tide shifts in the direction of more enlightened immigration and gender equality policies.

The often xenophobic insistence on racial purity is creating a climate in which it is difficult to become a Japanese national. Even when you are, you may be stripped of your passport if you choose to also become a citizen of another country. I know several cases cases of Japanese women who married foreign nationals and were stripped of their nationality for becoming citizens of the country in which they now live. How dare they adopt another nationality; don't they feel proud to be Japanese?

This deep-seated grappling with identity and racial purity was also in full view with Naomi Osaka's phenomenal success in tennis. For a time ranked no. 1 in the world, having won the US and then the Australian Open, Osaka is a *hafu* (Japanese mother, Haitian father). She was raised in New York (now lives in Florida) and while she holds a Japanese passport, she'll be compelled by law to choose (when she turns 22) whether she will continue to be Japanese. Perversely, dual citizenship is not an option in a country that is grappling with a demographic time bomb and is in need of in-migration to survive! The Japanese legal system (and public attitudes) has still not reconciled the nation's long-term survival (which may partly depend on relaxing citizenship legislation while becoming somewhat more welcoming of foreigners) and its insistence on national purity.

Interestingly, a *Japan Times* article (January 28, 2019) openly wondered *How Japanese is Naomi Osaka* on account of her background, upbringing, and behavior. In fact, some on social media saw her dignified conduct after her victory in the Melbourne final, as exemplifying her "Japaneseness" as if humility is a unique Japanese trait that can "even" offset her being black.

The Japanese model of economic organization (the "iron triangle" that's reliant on top-down economic direction, and close cooperation between big business, bureaucrats, and politicians) may need to be revisited. A mix of low fertility, low immigration, and low consumer spending has actually shrunk the economy over the last two decades (Milton, 2015).

Japan may lead the world in high-tech toilets, but this factoid may be indicative of a real problem for the country's fast-ageing society (*kōreika shakai*) that is expected to soon become the world's first "ultra-aged" country (defined as having 28% of the population in the over-65 bracket). As it stands today, it has a population of 127 million, roughly 27% of which is over 65. A bill has recently been proposed in the *Diet* that would allow two classes of labor to be imported into Japan by granting visas to 1) the younger and broader backs needed in the construction industry for short-term stays and 2) work permits for longer stays for those in professions or high-tech industries. Already, a number of convenience store franchisees with typically low-profit margins are using "guest workers" from countries like Nepal and Bangladesh. A third category, now under closer supervision, are so-called "training programs," abused by employers who use imported labor for work below the low minimum wage which no Japanese would accept. The scheme is also used by (often Asian) residents. The immigrants from Myanmar or rural China, however, often overstay the time specified on the visa and disappear or use the temporary permits to seek treatment for illness under the generous and comprehensive Japanese health system without having previously paid into it.

A more recent but related time bomb is a declining birth rate, now below replacement levels. A common complaint is the lack of inexpensive day-care centers for pre-kindergarten children, which would allow the distaff side of young families to return to the workforce as productive female members of society. Waiting lists are long. Hence, after giving birth, women are often able to secure only part-time employment in Japan. A recent suggestion, complicated by the costs of insurance and fear of mutual contamination by disease, would be to attach day-care centers to the burgeoning care facility industry dedicated to warehousing and rehabilitating the aged.

As I noted earlier, among Japan's future challenges is its education system. It's a very high standard, in many respects, but needs to permit more creativity, on top of strong numeracy and reasoning skills. Also, improving foreign language proficiency is a must in an age that is increasingly global and involves constant interactions across geographies. This will allow Japan to stay abreast of its aggressive Asian neighbors, especially China and Korea but this will not be possible without more emphasis on innovation. In an age where robots will most likely take over routine and process-based jobs, innovation and creativity (more of our right-brain) will become increasingly important.

Most of us in the West would stress that making mistakes and taking chances (and calculated risks) is the only way to break molds and create breakthroughs — not exactly the traditional way Japanese schools operate. This must certainly change, as society tries to tackle weighty challenges in a world that is increasingly unpredictable.

Sustainable environmental policies are another challenge. Japan's industrial base has led to a steep increase in greenhouse gases. Climate change is a serious issue, as it is for the rest of the world and then some. The country has already seen an increase in extreme rainfall events, and the average annual frequency of mudslides due to heavy rain and flooding has increased dramatically. The Japanese government has projected a fourfold increase in the likelihood of river flooding at the end of this century. Finally, Japan has invested heavily in nuclear power (as much as 30% of Japan's power was supplied by nuclear at the time of the 2011 tsunami) but as a small island nation fraught with volcanic activity, this decision has looked increasingly risky. After Fukuoka, the number of nuclear reactors has fallen from 54 to about 5, with others still undergoing inspection.

Social Cohesion: Too Much of a Good Thing?

Globalization carries many positives, not least of which is the breaking down of prejudices and social barriers, especially when the dominant values are those of liberalism: of tolerance, pluralism, and equality. It opens the door to the cross-fertilization of ideas, the spread of democracy and progressive ideas. On the other hand, it gives rise to inevitable tensions, when prevailing norms and tribal identities are challenged, until a new equilibrium is reached.

No doubt, the cohesion one observes in Japan, even though one can point to its downside of excluding outsiders, can be attributed to a fairly uniform culture and its attendant norms. It may also be at least partly attributable to a set of common values that influence governance. Take the justice system, for instance, which is perceived to be both fair and balanced. The "Lady with the Scales" is as balanced in Japan as it is anywhere in the world, albeit may err on the side of excessive rigor. Indeed, the system is equal in its administration as are universal health care and university admission.

Then there are certain forms of community building and civic participation associated with neighborhood policing that tend to raise eyebrows among some of my foreign acquaintances, not used to the "intrusiveness" of certain practices. A friend of mine recounted his experience with such regular visits, his Jewish background introducing a particularly interesting perspective:

At unpredictable intervals, but at least annually, two policemen appear at our door in Kyoto with a large bound blue ledger for amended entries. Having grown up as a secular Jew in a small East Texas community, the presence of the heavy jackboots at the door ("we've got you in our files") could only imply either real or imaginary guilt. Instead of feeling threatened by the Japanese equivalent of "neighborhood policing," I felt partially assimilated into a community in which every resident, regardless of residential status, age, or nationality, has a home visit from the neighborhood police at unannounced intervals. This periodic re-introduction differs from dependency in emergencies. As with other imaginable life-partners, transgression and communal affection are not so easily distinguishable.

Indeed, most foreign residents come to accept these visits for what they are: attempts at ensuring that everything is in order and the community is kept safe. The officers introduce themselves (with obligatory exchange of name cards) and proceed with questions: 1) confirmation of the owner and occupants of the house; 2) changes in the address and phone numbers of next-of-kin to be notified in the event of disaster or emergency; 3) a reminder of the communal assembly point for residents in the event of natural disaster; 4) the number and location of the nearest kooban (police box) to notify of any suspicious activity in the neighborhood; 5) informal inquiries as to my status as a resident in Japan; and 6) warnings of a neighborhood telephone scam targeting seniors. They then depart with a bow: community information sharing taking on the form of mutually benign profiling.

Then there are the quasi-mandatory Sunday morning assembly meetings with residents and neighborhood fire station representatives for an explanation of new fire extinguishers with complicated differences in design and application. One is to be used on electrical fires, the other on (usually *tempura*) oil or kerosene stoves used for winter heating in Japan. Each resident takes his supervised turn in storing, activating, and using each device. Later, the use of newly-installed AED devices is patiently explained with guided, time-consuming individual trials on fiberglass mannequins.

During the question period, an octogenarian asks how you apply the device to someone who lives with a pacemaker and how you "feel" for it, a reminder of the "ageing" society in which many of us have a share.

During such events, residents are expected to temporarily abandon freedoms characteristic of other Sunday mornings, although some may see these directed activities as the intrusions of a nanny state into citizens" privacy and free time. Building community is not without its nuisances.

There is, of course, the occasional resistance to these bureaucratic intrusions. Given an ageing population, the fire department once requested approval for periodic inspection of household appliances, wiring, smoke detectors, exhaust fans, and automated cut-off devices, without providing a schedule. Occupants unanimously rejected the free service, on the grounds that, because unannounced, they would have no time to clean up the house for quasi-official "guests." Could there be a better affirmation of the distinction made long ago by Ruth Benedict, between Japan as a shame culture and our guilt culture? In attempting shared incremental improvement, we each often mess up in unpredictable, yet retrospectively logical ways, usually open to explanation, if subjected to testing.

Japan is a country known for its attention to incrementally ameliorative detail in industrial products, design, cuisine, and handicraft. Hence, timely steps to improve the quality of collective life (a form of "just in time" delivery of service parts to the aged) initially seem "nefarious meddling," redundant, or necessary only to the self-maintenance of a bureaucracy with too much time on its hands. Or, as in Japan's industrial penchant for intriguing incremental tweaks to existing products patented elsewhere (temperature-controlled toilet seats), they could well represent an alternative wall against open access, known as collective protectionism against which the West rails. Opportunistic employment, however, is not inconsistent with well-being. A culture of incremental improvement (*kaizen*) reveals Japanese humility and curiosity in the face of challenges and the flexibility to discontinue a suggestion or mandate if it proves ineffective, cannot be verified as an improvement, or lacks acceptance because of some unforeseen local condition. Pragmatic, incremental steps are conjunctive: we learn how we "got that way." They enhance both patience to wait for the results and further inventive fudging along the edges to make life better for all. Will it work, how can it be improved, what support does it have, and does the support bring us closer?

This knowledge now informs the belated recognition that small, collectively negotiated footsteps, both literally and metaphorically, may more readily represent and activate nuanced civic participation, because they teach and test.

When I first considered the inclusion of these experiences in my exploration of Japanese culture, I thought that few in the West would ever understand both the mild rule of law and community participation that is described as routine in Japan. In America or Europe, "the law" only comes to your door when you have committed an offense rather than as part of a constant sharing of information among fellow citizens in the neighborhood. But then again, applying that standard, I may have opted to remove many hard to comprehend passages, lest I baffle the reader who has not yet been exposed to this wonderful, yet complex culture. In the end, I opted for a dose of raw tidbits that make up the fascinating kaleidoscope of cultural idiosyncrasies that characterize Japan.

Environmental Threats

I have touched upon the reverence for nature as one of the dominant themes in Japanese literature, from an early animistic conception to later views of man-nature harmony, co-existence and the environment as a source of incredible (albeit fleeting) beauty. Indeed, the environment occupies a special place in the Japanese psyche, one that finds expression in many facets of its culture, especially in literature. Yet that strong link has been tested of late in ways that have created a profound re-evaluation of Japan's emphasis on economic progress (and the urbanization and industrialization that underpin it) at the expense of virtually everything else. For Murakami and other Japanese intellectuals, our direct connection with nature has been long lost to urbanization and now exists only inside us.

The Fukushima Daiichi nuclear power disaster may have been the most high-profile environmental threat but it is hard to reconcile what one sees in modern Japan from the idealized image of man-nature harmony underlying much of the Japanese aesthetic. There is little aesthetic beauty in the concrete slabs one sees in Japanese cities or along the industrialized coast. High-density living no doubt requires compromise but it does not have to lead to concrete jungles, cacophonous neon signs and pachinko parlors.

Industrialization and urbanization took their toll as the Japanese focused on a version of modernization that put the interests of industry ahead of its people and their natural habitat. Nature came to be viewed as something to be controlled and subjugated, a subversive attitude that ran roughshod over traditional sensibilities. That the majority was largely complacent in the face of bureaucratic decisions favoring those who would later provide cushy contracts (see *amakudari*) owes much to the collectivist ethos and its tolerance of authority.

Fortunately, even if belatedly, there have been efforts to address some of the most serious environmental issues at all levels—government, corporate as well as individuals. On the government level, the Ministry of Environment (established in 2001) is making an effort to reduce air emissions, water usage, and municipal waste. At the corporate level, most large corporations have reacted to public concern over environmental degradation and climate change with corporate social responsibility initiatives. Toyota, for example, established the *Toyota Environmental Challenge 2050* that aims to counter global warming through zero CO_2 emissions. Another goal it has set, is to sell at least 5.5million electrified vehicles annually by 2030. Other corporations have followed suit with a variety of CSR initiatives to the extent that Japanese corporations are now at the forefront of environmental scorecards and CSR reporting. The Global Reporting Initiative (GRI) provides a set of economic, environmental, and social performance standards and Japanese corporations have been among the most committed adopters globally. Only time will tell whether sustainability efforts prove to be successful but the first step is always the commitment to action in meaningful ways: in the selection of supply chain partners based on specific sustainability criteria; complementing financial reporting with metrics that include broader sustainability goals; and holding political as well as business leadership accountable for the results. A commitment which on the face of it is evident at all levels of Japanese society: government, industry and the broader community.

Chapter 12

Unique or Distinctive?

Any exploration of a complex culture such as Japan's is prone to oversimplification. My aim was not to dissect it in an exhaustive manner, but rather examine it from various perspectives, or lenses, that allow the reader to gain fresh insight into the assumptions, perspectives, shared values, and accepted behavior that it embodies. The more time I spent away from my own culture, the more I gained an understanding of what it takes to successfully navigate life among people who have been brought up with distinctly different frames of reference. It requires getting outside one's own comfort zone, keeping an open mind and showing empathy for different perspectives. What is more, I became passably adept at deciphering the cues that would allow me to "be allowed in."

The lenses I've chosen offer different angles or perspectives through which to view Japanese culture and society, yet are often reflected in the other lenses. In that sense, perhaps the kaleidoscope metaphor would also be appropriate in that it is an instrument that, when we turn it or look at it through a different light, the scene changes, but still has residues of what we have already seen.

Naturally, geography has always played a vital role in the way in which Japanese culture evolved, and the characteristics regarded as fundamental to its very essence. The ability to "adopt, adapt, and then become adept" is certainly one of its key sources of enduring dynamism, as the Japanese have gone about learning from other cultures while retaining (and often reframing) their own distinct qualities.

This begs the question: Is Japanese culture truly unique or merely distinctive? I'm firmly in the camp of those who prefer to use the term distinctive, even though it may be true that many Japanese cultural traits are rather unique in the way they're configured or expressed. This is far from suggesting that they are somehow new to the human condition as the proponents of *nihonjin-ron* would have us believe. It's one thing to say that the Greeks have a very nuanced way of expressing different aspects of what we may broadly call "love" (making the distinction between *eros, agape,* and *pathos* not articulated that finely in other languages). But it's another to suggest that somehow this sets the culture apart from all others in terms of understanding this fundamental human state. Similarly, the Japanese have words that express complex psychological states such as *amaeru* (indulgent love) or *giri* (obligation), in more subtle and nuanced ways than through our own linguistic prism. Yet it doesn't mean that such feelings aren't present, even if not as well articulated through our native vocabularies.

Innumerable books have been written on Japan, partly reflecting the West's fascination with the country, but also perhaps showing a misplaced sense among the Japanese themselves that they are uniquely different, which explains the vast amount of ink spilled by Japanese authors exploring their own identity (*nihonjin-ron*). As you recall, in our discussion on the language lens, there is a specific word, *amakudari*, which means "direct descent from heaven." It is hard to find a nation that suffers from a larger delusion, although one can see some parallels in American exceptionalism ("God shed his grace on thee," Emerson's "indispensable nation"). The image of a city upon a hill—uniquely favored by the Almighty and a light unto the heathens—is a popular image of America, shared by many distinguished visitors such as Alexis de Tocqueville who declared it "exceptional" as well as unique and special. Indeed, there were overt references to the divine basis for this in Abraham Lincoln's Gettysburg Address:

> *We here highly resolve that these dead shall not have died in vain— that this nation, under God, shall have a new birth of freedom— and that government of the people, by the people, for the people, shall not perish from the earth.*

Of course, there are also scholars who view the EU as *sui generis*, representing a "Hegelian moment…that has no current analogies…unique in the world as an experiment in political integration" (Hoffman, 2011). So, if one examines the history of nations or a confederate supra-national organization (such as the EU) through the narratives associated with their genesis, they are perhaps not so "exceptional" even if nations such as Japan (and the US) have made the argument a central tenet of their very identity. This reminds me of a discussion I had with a professor friend of mine regarding the possible differences between Japanese and American exceptionalism. We concluded that the latter is largely "conjunctive"—an exceptionalism that presumes a universality (all people are equal, anyone can be President, self-determination, no class consciousness). Indeed, this may strike some as counterintuitive. The presumption is that everyone will want to have a share in its central tenets and therefore has an aspirational (uniting and universal) appeal. Japanese exceptionalism on the other hand may be more "disjunctive" with implied barriers, some known and some unknown (language, formal social codes, protectionism) so it tends to imply separation rather than uniting.

It could of course be said that our fascination with Japan's distinctiveness makes eminent sense since it was the first country beyond the West to buck conventional wisdom that non-Western economies couldn't possibly outcompete those of the US and Europe. How could non-Westerners build products the rest of the world wanted? Japan disproved the myth that this wasn't possible. In fact, the more Japanese products outshone Western ones, even in premium and luxury segments, the more "emulation-worthy" and *chic* Japan became as a conversation topic.

Domestic fascination with identity and difference, on the other hand, was mainly the result of the Japanese proclivity for introspection but also of the tendency to confound the notion of "nation" with that of a shared culture. Taking that idea a step further, this preoccupation took the form of arguments for defining their own "tribe" on the basis of ethnicity and race or even in primordial terms (the origin from which their achievements derive their provenance). So, while a dose of introspection is healthy, it easily veers toward a compulsion to prove Japan's "uniqueness" in a way that borders on cultural nationalism. Indeed, *nihonjin-ron* dwells on Japan's supposed "uniqueness" in linguistic, sociological, and philosophical terms, papering over any socio-historical diversity that no doubt exists. Japan is not really unique in attempting to buttress the fiction of sovereignty by strategically eliding nativity, country, state, and mythic origins to maintain the idea of difference and uniqueness. Of course, scientific evidence suggests that we are all descended from Africa if we look far enough into the past. Move the frame of reference (from 100,000 years to several thousand) and the early Japanese who came to the archipelago were a mix of Ainu, Polynesian, Central Asian, and Manchu-Korean—hardly genetically "pristine." What is more, science tells us that any two humans differ, on average, at about 1 in 1,000 DNA base pairs (0.1%) making the human genetic diversity substantially lower than that of many other species (including that of our closest cousins, the chimpanzees). So much for the idea that race represents real biological differences.

In his book *The Myth of Japanese Uniqueness*, Peter Dale (2012) describes the rationale for *nihonjin-ron* as follows:

> *First, they implicitly assume that the Japanese constitute a culturally and socially homogeneous racial entity, whose essence is virtually unchanged from prehistoric times down to the present day. Secondly, they presuppose that the Japanese differ radically from all other known peoples. Thirdly, they are conspicuously nationalistic, displaying a conceptual and procedural hostility to any mode of analysis, which might be seen to derive from external, non-Japanese sources.*

Of course, no one who truly understands the Japanese or has lived in Japan will deny that there are traits which make Japanese culturally very distinct. But the same can be said (although one may argue about the degree) of Chinese, Indian, or other discrete cultures (or their strong subcultures). Thus, while cross-cultural studies are useful when based on impartial evidence and insight, they can be misleading and superficial when they're designed to validate preconceived notions that propagate exceptionalism.

For me, one of the most interesting features of Japanese culture is how it manages to blend or accommodate apparent opposites, being both pioneering and conventional, feminine and masculine, flexible yet firm, simultaneously. For lack of a better term, I refer to this as the *yin* and *yang*, the delicate balance of *ikebana*, form and space, a dynamic brilliantly explored by Ruth Benedict, an American anthropologist, in her classic, *The Chrysanthemum and the Sword*. Written during World War II, for use by the US War Department, the book is one of the most insightful ever written on Japanese society and culture. Yet, its author never visited Japan (tricky when it's wartime!) and relied on extensive interviews with Japanese living in the US.

According to Benedict, the Japanese are, to the highest degree, both aggressive and unaggressive, both militaristic and aesthetic, both insolent and polite, rigid and adaptable, submissive and resentful of being pushed around, loyal and treacherous, brave and timid, conservative and hospitable to new ways. They are very concerned about what other people think of their behavior but may also feel guilt when other people know nothing of their misstep (although this does not go as far as an internalized conviction of sin).

Of course, Benedict was trying to be nuanced in her approach and avoid simple stereotyping:

> *Certainly, I found that once I had seen where my Occidental assumptions did not fit into their view of life and had got some idea of the categories and symbols they used, many contradictions Westerners are accustomed to seeing in Japanese behavior were no longer contradictions.*

To this, I would add the apparent contradiction of being both detached from and being enthralled with Western culture. *Taigan no Kaji* is a Japanese proverb that encapsulates a calculated reticence that strongly characterizes Japanese culture. It conveys, "a passivity induced by far away events with which I do not allow myself to be troubled." This reticence or detachment can be juxtaposed to its fascination with all things Western and the active attempt to absorb, learn from, and experience other cultures, especially those (see Western) they see as advanced.

An offshoot of the argument on uniqueness or distinctiveness is inevitably the attempt to place the Japanese ahead of or behind the West. I recall the conversations I had with foreign friends living in Japan on this very topic with arguments to support both conclusions. The non-acceptance of an American institution (the Mall), now being destroyed en masse as tastes change (Walmart has gone bankrupt twice in Japan) may point to an innate knack for sensing enduring trends. Indeed, Japan seems more enamored of the arcades projects celebrated by Walter Benjamin, as one may witness from walking through identically covered passageways ubiquitous in even small towns in Japan, euphemistically known as "Ginzas." Or take the concepts of "scaling" and "customization" and you'll find solutions that incorporate customer preferences into product design in truly novel ways. There is a company in Kyoto that makes a lovely auto body, a kind of retro shape like detective Colombo's old Peugeot (remember the TV series?) but with flowing lines resembling Karmann Ghias from the '70s. You then order the engine you want (from Toyota, Honda, or Nissan, in conventional or electric hybrid versions) and they fit it to the auto chassis. You pay for the engine performance you want (in terms of cubic centimeters), so that the engine becomes an option, like wire wheels. That would be like the Boeing 787 Dreamliner: you can order GE engines or a Rolls Royce Trent engine depending upon routes, performance, weight, and maintenance demands while on the ground. You break down Henry Ford's assembly line (the quintessential industrial innovation) and allow the consumer a role in not merely the design, but the performance parameters. That carries the notion of "fitting" to a new level. A wholly different example that may also indicate a knack of "seeing ahead" is the high proportion of Japanese women (around 10%) who never marry. It is one of the highest in the world! What used to be an anomaly, perhaps, is seen the world over: unmarried women harvesting their eggs in the event they can never find a husband or don't want one. Again, perhaps Japan was ahead, rather than behind.

Anecdotal evidence of being ahead of the curve (or lagging behind) notwithstanding, Japan has shown a remarkable ability to deal with the challenges it has faced, often as a collective to assimilate and adapt. This without losing sight of the underlying principles and shared values the society has held dear. Take, for instance, the tendency toward restrained materialism, which is evident in chronically low consumption and high savings rates.

146

It is also evident in the eschewing of ostentatious displays of wealth. The rich in Japan tend to avoid showing off their wealth (in the houses they live, the cars they drive, and the yachts they *don't* possess) save the tendency to purchase expensive luxury brands such as Louis Vuitton and Prada. This dignified restraint (combined perhaps with a dose of spirituality) appealed to many in the West as a social model that manages to better reconcile the tensions between the individual and the collective or between commercialism and spirituality—the latter term not in the sense of religious dogma but in the broader sense of a reverence of nature and the wonders of the cosmos.

Seen from this perspective, Marie Kondo's "clean up your life" philosophy and its "dematerialization" seems to have struck a chord among many across the world who seek to find a better balance between the material and the spiritual. This may very well be a sustaining value within Japanese culture, which seems to resonate more in times of increasing global volatility and uncertainty.

Indeed, what one might term "inconspicuous consumption" strikes me as one of the many apparent contradictions in the culture when seen through the prism of luxury brand consumption and what it normally signifies. For me, one of the continuing delights about Japan is the relative absence of materialism(s). Few of the friends I've known have a strong interest in amassing wealth, or even "entrepreneurship." These are doctors, professors, consultants, lawyers, and artists. Compared with my ambitious British, Greek, or Cypriot bankers, consultants and professors, they seem relatively immune from the all-consuming desire for added wealth. Is it because their basic needs are covered (Marie Kondo's Zen-like doctrine of "minimalization") or something else altogether? They seem not to want a life much better than what they have. But in the West, the "desire" to be much better off or richer is what binds Trump's populism to the poor soul in Ohio who has lost his job at GM, the farmer who can't sell his soybeans because China is buying them from Brazil, or the professor in California who wants to be Provost. Of course, we all want more (wealth, fame, success) but we're talking about a matter of degree here (as well as what we are willing to give up in pursuing such a goal).

Yes, the Japanese enjoy a good meal and women do spend on high fashion and I even knew someone in Kyoto with a Monet oil painting. But the whole economy is not 70% private consumption as it is in the US (it actually hovers around a relatively modest 55%). Is it some natural thriftiness or contentment with the status quo? There is no "Black Friday" shopping madness, as there is in the US or, lately, in most Western economies. In fact, no one seems to talk about money in Japan. In the US, Singapore, China, or Cyprus where I live, people ask how much you paid for something without hesitation or any feeling of bad manners. Japanese rarely talk about how much "X" paid for his house in a luxury neighborhood—which tends to be cocktail conversation elsewhere. Whether or not it is a middle-class country, people certainly behave as if it is. This is not nor will it perhaps ever be addressed in business schools, but maybe it should be.

I've debated this point with a friend of mine (long-time resident of Japan) and I found myself able to argue for or against the "materialistic" proposition. If the Japanese are not as materialistic as we are in the West, why then is their fixation on luxury goods so pronounced?

Well, my hypothesis is that it has less to do with Veblen's notion of conspicuous consumption and more to do with a desire to associate oneself with exclusivity and discerning taste. The product's symbolic characteristics or "heritage" provides a boost to our very identify and self-worth. This can be "socially" driven (of what it signifies about us within our social circles) but it can also be a largely intrinsic motivation, which is perhaps the more important driver in Japanese culture. A case in point is a woman from Kyoto who purchased three expensive *Qum* carpets from a dealer in the UK, only to display them in her own home where even her close family friends were not privy to the "acquisition." An inward association with our identity and self-worth (a product's influence on our self-image) is not typically why we buy expensive luxury items in the West. Indeed, display is seeking the judgment of others about one's commercial tastes, and the Japanese seem not to need that form of confirmation.

Consumption mostly driven by intrinsic motivation (to strengthen self-esteem) is one side of the coin. The other, is a traditional tendency among Japanese to avoid risk. This combined with a very high savings rate might suggest that as a generalization, the Japanese are cautious and risk averse. A number of American brokerage houses attempted to tap the huge Japanese household savings pool through affiliations with Japanese banks in the period from 2006–2009 (not the best timing) but failed to generate any real traction. Most of these, including Merrill-Lynch and Citibank, quickly withdrew from the attempt to sell equities, bonds, REITs, and other investment products to Japanese customers. The aversion to assets perceived as potentially risky may partially explain the persistence of investments in inflated local real estate (*fudōsan*, "immovable assets"). It may also explain the "investment" in *omiai* ("arranged marriages") whereby the traditional convention avoids the presumably heightened inflationary and deflationary risks of short-term passion while allowing history (in the form of parental approvals and guarantees) a role in "rating" the investment that is marriage.

As the perceptive reader might note, my thoughts on the topic are sufficiently speculative to include a familiar cautionary note before investment in the idea: past results are no guarantee of future returns.

The ability to blend opposites and adapt to changing conditions does not translate to anything resembling smooth transitions. It does produce disequilibria which are hopefully temporary. One can't help but think that Japanese modernization and its focus on growth at all costs, took its toll and has created some of the evident societal dysfunctions I have discussed in this book. The compulsive drive to compete and dominate can be seen as induced more by a desire to grow and succeed, even at the expense of the environment or social balance and cohesion. Japanese culture has indeed shown remarkable resilience but there are elements of the social, economic, and political fabric that have become problematic. Many had expected the nation's trajectory to be different in terms of power and relevance, yet there is no doubt that some of the more optimistic predictions appeared premature. Excessive bureaucracy, an educational system that stresses conformity (over originality) and is ill-adapted to the needs of the 21st century as well as a demographically skewed social fabric, are all restraining factors that may render Japan less relevant (and consequential) on the world stage.

As I reflect on my own experiences, I feel privileged for being "allowed in," to share in the experiences that constitute "Japaneseness." The Greek notion of *filoxenia* denotes being a "friend" (*filos*) to a "stranger" (*xenos*) yet this is often mis-construed as an unconditional, absolute, extension of hospitality. But that is not so in most cultural contexts, and certainly not in Japan. Being granted hospitality is never totally unconditional and for those brought up in low-context cultures, the cues may be particularly hard to decipher. While presenting a façade of hospitality (in *tatemae* terms) they are in fact "kept out" (through *honne*) without their even knowing.

Understanding Japan requires curiosity, humility, and a dose of caution, made more difficult when conditioned in cultures that pride themselves on the ease of assimilation, high-context directness, and explicit cues, showing little tolerance for constructive ambiguity. Hence, the question as to Japan's legendary uniqueness and whether or not this makes it truly different (which would limit accessibility to natives) may be problematic, though a question worth asking. We may need help in meeting the "stranger" in the same way that the first-time reader might need a collection of essays and/or a professor of long experience and reflective lenses to guide him to a fuller understanding of Joyce's formal and thematic interests. On a second or third "reading," what had at first seemed forbidding or bizarre assumes the familiarity that accompanies the surprise of an *apercu* which may strike suddenly as an emergent *interest*.

Alternatively, we may "like it," but not be able to explain why we like it—the irrationality of the new lover. I want to see and experience more of it! Let us take two examples from social practices in cultures that are relative strangers. Finland (with an allegedly very difficult language) is well known for its exterior and interior design. Aalto, Saarinen, and Nordic furniture have had a historically wide appeal for clean lines and efficient use of space. For such a small and relatively new country, the number of designers and architects is extraordinary. One explanation (offered by a local architect) was that in a very cold country without much natural light for over half the year, the capturing and preservation of light and heat (the first functional solar-powered house is in Finland) became a key feature of interior and exterior design theory and practice. The French impressionists captured fleeting sunlight on paper and canvas using different techniques and materials including pointillism and later, Van Gogh's myth of the sunflowers. Is Nordic interior design a corollary to the same interest that assumed a different socio-cultural direction? I have no idea, except a rationalization for what we have come to love, but we needed the "lens" of cultural "skylights," to enlighten us: the *nakahodo*, a professional intermediary.

A second example should suffice. In all countries, loss as a consequence of the death of a loved one or family member is deeply heartfelt. Coping with grief assumes the historical formats discussed so intelligently by Phillipe Aries in *The Hour of Our Death*. One practice in Japan brings forth more than tears and fears. With its high population density and exorbitant prices for land, cremation and burial in the family vault is efficient, economical, and a marvelous space-saver. The officiating cleric (most die as at least titular Buddhists in Japan) and the family follow the hearse to the crematorium for the final prayers before the body is committed to the flames. Usually, there are other cremations being conducted at the same time and the oldest survivor takes a number and awaits the "delivery" of the earthly remains, usually within an hour. The funeral director then wheels out the still-smoking remains on its gurney and points out the thigh bone, part of the skull, and the hardened ash of a knee cap amidst the smoldering powder. He then hands each member of the family a set of chopsticks and in turn, the surviving family members "partake." Each chooses and deposits a morsel of the deceased into an urn to be interred behind one of the stones in the family vault after a prescribed "decent interval" during which a symbolic vegetarian repast is set out nightly to sustain the soul on its journey to numerous reincarnations. For those with only intermediate chopstick skills, you might want to choke them slightly before proceeding to avoid embarrassing drops.

The practice could be described as simultaneously bizarre, totally different, genuinely unique, or even barbaric. For me, a totally new and frightening experience during which my only thought (other than the grip on the chopsticks) was the schism in Christianity that occurred over a disputation upon whether or not the wafer and wine consumed during the Eucharist was the real body and blood of Christ or only symbolic. Both are implicated in a *wakeru*, a division that is a re-distribution.

Afterword

All cultures, as constructions of collective identity, have their own essence, forms, and rhythm of development, marked by critical historical events. As I conclude my reflections on Japan, I therefore wonder how the mysterious inaccessibility nurtured by the Japanese in the form of various "non-structural barriers" is a unique way of preserving sovereignty in a country that lost it rather dramatically in 1945 and lacks a strong military deterrent (usually a necessary tool) in order to preserve it.

The nature of culture is cultivation, and the physical, linguistic, and economic barriers I have attempted to de-code or illuminate make logical sense (i.e., they are part of the culture) in a country that suffered a loss of sovereignty so dramatically and would have been in danger of becoming a "client state" after an unconditional surrender (remember, Germany did not surrender unconditionally).

The uniqueness abates with exposure, re-reading, and reflection as we apply different lenses with which to interrogate our own beliefs. The need to continually re-read cultures as we re-read novels or even relationships reflects a world that changes as we ourselves change. Of course, we sometimes read incorrectly or without sufficient evidence; hence the lenses reflect the object, the world, and our "place" in it. That is *sumimasen* writ large.

If we approach this exposure in ways that are open-minded, iterative, and dialectic (rather than as means to impose our own views, and persuade others) we may broaden our intellectual horizons, shedding light on the beliefs and values by which we live our own lives. This interrogation never stops even at the end (of our books as well as us). "Epilogues" or "Afterwords," too, are provisional in Japan. *Sumimasen* ("we have not yet finished").

Bibliography

Baron, N., Hard, Y. (2010). "Cross-cultural patterns in mobile phone use: Public space and reachability in Sweden, the US, and Japan." New Media & Society, February 2010, 12(1).

Chu, B. (2018, December 23). Carlos Ghosn may be guilty—but the Japanese criminal justice system is in the dock too. [online] Independent.

Condry, I. (2013). The Soul of Anime: Collaborative Creativity and Japan's Media Success Story. Durham and London: Duke University Press.

Cusumano, M. A. (1985). The Japanese Automobile Industry: Technology and Management at Nissan and Toyota. Cambridge, MA: Council on East Asian Studies, Harvard University.

Dale, P. (2012). The Myth of Japanese Uniqueness. (Routledge Revivals) 1st Edition

Doi, T. (2001). The anatomy of dependence. Tokyo; New York: Kodansha International.

Dunbar, R (2010) How Many Friends Does One Person Need? Dunbar's Number and Other Evolutionary Quirks, Harvard University Press.

Edahiro, J. (2015, January 24). Toward a Sustainable Japan: Challenges and Changes in Society and Population. [online] Our World.

Edwards, M. (2015, September 9). Why Japan's Sumo Culture is in Crisis. [online] Highsnobiety.

Ezrati, M. (2015, March 25). The Demographic Time Bomb Crippling Japan's Economy. [online] The National Interest.

Galbraith, P. (2014). The Otaku Encyclopedia: An Insider's Guide to the Subculture of Cool Japan. Kodansha.

Gladwell, M. (2008). Outliers: The Story of Success. New York: Little,

Brown & Co.

Gordon, J. (1996). "Preface." Gossip and Subversion in Nineteenth-Century British Fiction: Echo's Economies. Basingstoke and New York: Macmillan and St. Martin's, p. xiii.

Hahn, E. (1983), An Overview of the Japanese Legal System, Northwest Journal of Int'l Law & Business, no. 517.

Hall, E. T. (1976). Beyond Culture. Garden City, NY: Anchor Press.

Hanauer, D. (2001). Focus on Cultural Understanding: Literary Reading in the Second Language Classroom. Cauce: Revista de Filología y su Didactica, no 24.

Hernon, M. (2016). Tormented Talents: The Darker Side of Japan's Entertainment Biz. [online] Tokyo Weekender. (Dec. 2)

Hincks, J. (2017, January 30). This Japanese Slot Game Generates More Revenue Than Las Vegas and Macau Combined. [online] Fortune.

Hoffman, L. (2011) Becoming Exceptional? American and European Exceptionalism and their Critics: Review, L'Europe En Formation 2011/1, no 359.

Hofstede, G. (2001). Culture's Consequences: comparing values, behaviors, institutions, and organizations across nations (2nd ed.). Thousand Oaks, CA: SAGE Publications.

Inagami, T., Whittaker H. (2005). The New Community Firm: Employment, Governance and Management Reform in Japan. Cambridge University Press.

JETRO: Japan External Trade Organization—Economic Research Department. (2005). "Cool" Japan's Economy Warms Up. [online]

Kakuzō, O. (1906). The Book of Tea. New York: Duffield & Co.

Kaplan, D., Dubro, A. (2012). Yakuza: Japan's criminal underworld. 25th-anniversary edition. University of California Press.

Kelts, R. (2013, May 9). Lost in Translation, The New Yorker.

Komiya, N. (1999). "A cultural study of the low crime rate in Japan." The British Journal of Criminology, Volume 39, Issue 3 (1 June 1999), pp. 369–390.

Kondo, M. (2014) The Life-Changing Magic of Tidying: A simple, effective way to banish clutter forever. Vermilion.

Krastev, I. (2017, January 18). "The Rise and Fall of European Meritocracy." The International New York Times, p. 14.

Kyodo News Agency. (2018, January 18). Japan's crime rate hits record low as number of thefts plummets. Japan Times.

Ladd, F., & Deneroff, H. (2009). Astro Boy and Anime Come to the Americas: An insider's view of the birth of a pop culture phenomenon. Jefferson: McFarland & Company Inc.

Levy, M. J. Jr. (2000). "Some Implications of Japanese Social Structure," The American Sociologist, Vol. 31, No. 2, pp. 18–31.

McCurry, J. (2011, July 13). Fukishima cleanup recruits "nuclear gypsies" from across Japan. [online] The Guardian.

McGray, D. (2009) Japan's Gross National Cool, Foreign Policy (November 11).

McIlroy, J. (2017, November 1). Why Japan may be the world's next car superpower. [online] CNN.

Moon, K. (2018, November 15). The Korean CSAT is the exam that stops a nation. BBC.

Morin, R. (2017, November 7). How to Hire Fake Friends and Family. The Atlantic.

Morris, I. (1975). The Nobility of Failure: Tragic Heroes in the History of Japan. New York: Holt, Rinehart and Winston.

Nye, J. S. (2005). Soft Power: The Means To Success In World Politics. New York: Public Affairs.

Osono, E. Shimizu, N. Takeuchi, H. (2008). Extreme Toyota: Radical Contradictions That Drive Success at the World's Best Manufacturer. Wiley.

Ozyurtcu, T. (2017, July 10). Wrestling With Tradition: Mongolia, Japan and the Changing Face of Sumo. Stratfor.

Randolph, L. (2015, April 30). How Sushi Became an American Institution. Paste Magazine.

Renton, A. (2006, February 26). How sushi ate the world. [online] The Guardian.

Rose, A. (2015). Like Me, Buy Me: The Effect of Soft Power on Exports. NBER Working Paper No. 21537. (September)

Sehgal, P. (2011, October 21). Six Questions for Jay Rubin, Haruki Murakami's Translator. Publishers Weekly.

Simonitch, S. (2012, October 3). Japan's first "cuddle cafe" lets you sleep with a stranger for ¥6,000 an hour. Japan Today.

Sōseki, N. (1972). *I Am a Cat. Translated by Aiko Itō & Graeme Wilson.* Tokyo, Japan: Tuttle Publishing.

Takehiko, K. (2011). *"Credential inflation and employment in "universal" higher education: enrolment, expansion and (in)equity via privatisation in Japan." Journal of Education and Work, 24:1–2, 69–94.*

Talbot, M. (2002, December 15). *The Year in Ideas; Pokémon Hegemon. [online] The New York Times Magazine.*

Twomey, B. (2018, March 8). *Understanding Japanese Keiretsu. [online] Investopedia.*

van Ham, P. (2001). *"The Rise of the Brand State: The Postmodern Politics of Image and Reputation." Foreign Affairs, 80(5), 2-6.*

Yano, C. R. (2009). *"Wink on Pink: Interpreting Japanese Cute as It Grabs the Global Headlines." The Journal of Asian Studies. [online] 68(3), 681–688.*

YouMeSushi. (2014, August 28). *What Does it Take to Become a Sushi Chef? [online]*

ABOUT THE AUTHOR

Nicos Rossides is an accomplished CEO and organizational development consultant. Having studied in the US as a Fulbright scholar, he earned his doctorate in engineering from Japan's prestigious Kyoto University, where he studied as a *Mombusho* scholar. He later received his senior management training at MIT's Sloan School.

He lived in Japan for 7 years in the late '70s and early '80s, is married to a Japanese, and has frequently visited Japan since then on business as well as to visit friends and family.

Dr. Rossides is co-founder and Chairman of the Advisory Board of DigitalMR, an international digital marketing insights firm based in London. He also runs, as CEO, his own management consultancy firm, Rossides Associates. He was previously CEO of Synovate's CEEME region as well as its Head of Global Solutions, and CEO of Medochemie, a global generic pharmaceutical company.

Dr. Rossides currently devotes most of his time to writing, managing his management consulting company and his Boardroom duties.

For exclusive discounts on Matador titles,
sign up to our occasional newsletter at
troubador.co.uk/bookshop